Forgotten Fruit

*

THE ENGLISH ORCHARD
AND FRUIT GARDEN

Also by Francesca Greenoak

All the Birds of the Air:
the Names, Language and Lore of British Birds

Forgotten Fruit

THE ENGLISH ORCHARD
AND FRUIT GARDEN

◦⊢ · ⊣◦

Francesca Greenoak

Illustrated by Alastair Robertson

ANDRE DEUTSCH

FIRST PUBLISHED 1983 BY
ANDRE DEUTSCH LIMITED
105 GREAT RUSSELL STREET LONDON WC1

TYPESET BY GLOUCESTER TYPESETTING SERVICES
PRINTED IN GREAT BRITAIN BY
EBENEZER BAYLIS & SON LTD
THE TRINITY PRESS, WORCESTER, AND LONDON

ISBN 0 233 97396 6

To Alice and Howarth
who love fruit

Contents

❦ · ❧

List of illustrations

Author's note and acknowledgements

GARDENING WRITERS of the past believed that raising fruit brought out the best in human nature. In gathering information for this book, I talked to many nursery owners, gardeners and fruit specialists, and found them unfailingly patient and helpful. There are a few people to whom I owe particular thanks. Mr Harry Baker of the Royal Horticultural Society's Garden at Wisley not only corresponded generously but read and amended the final draft and gave invaluable judgements on the final section. Mr John Woodward guided me round the collection and library of the National Fruit Trials in the early days. Mr David Smith continued an enthusiastic and informative correspondence on the gooseberry. Writers and Readers Publishing Co-operative were kind enough to allow me to quote the passage from John Berger's *Pig Earth* published by them in 1979. Warm thanks also to John Kilpatrick and Richard Mabey for their unflagging kindness and help throughout.

I should also like to acknowledge a deep debt to two gardeners and writers whose work on the history of gardening I have found profoundly stimulating: The Hon. Alicia Amherst and Eleanour Sinclair Rohde.

During the last few decades, many traditional orchards have been grubbed up and replaced by alternative crops and large numbers of hedgerow fruit trees and bushes have been removed with the hedges themselves. There has been increasing anxiety among gardeners and orchardists who care about the old kinds of home-grown fruit that some of the historic varieties would be permanently lost. It is not the first time in history that people have been so concerned. In the late eighteenth century, Sir William Chambers feared that with the sweeping orchard clearances of those times, there would soon 'not be a fruit tree left standing in the whole kingdom'. The tide turned then, and I believe it is turning for us too.

In the process of tracing the histories of traditional fruit varieties, I have read books and documents from earliest times up to the present. It was with growing excitement that as I compared the last few issues of nursery catalogues, I observed that the choice of fruit is actually getting wider. It seems that once again gardeners are becoming interested in the traditional varieties. Paradoxically, the very characteristics which make a fruit uncommercial for mass marketing are the ones which recommend it to an individual gardener who desires not piles of standardized produce but variety, distinction and excellence.

It will not be the large commercial orchards which perpetuate the range of historic varieties, but ordinary people who grow fruit in their gardens and smallholdings, or even in courtyards and patios. Fruit can be grown successfully in so many forms: trees of all sizes from large to dwarf, fans and tiered espaliers, right down to tubs and pots. There is such a wide choice in fruit, form and flavour that everyone can fashion a fruit garden to their own individual taste and requirements.

In this short book, I have confined my attention to fruits known to have been grown over a long period in Britain and which were already being raised in gardens by the sixteenth century and in some cases long before that. This is a companion book for gardeners rather than a manual but I hope that readers will find useful the appended lists of practical gardening books and fruit specialists.

Wigginton 1981

Note I have left aside entirely one subject which greatly occupied the gardeners of the past, namely, grafting. This can still be done by amateurs and some nurseries supply materials and stocks for the purpose. It is, however, an area in which I have no personal experience and I think that most fruit gardeners today are content to leave this skilled task to expert hands.

CHAPTER ONE

Early Orchards

'What shall I say? A thousand pleasant delights are attending on an Orchard: and the sooner shall I be weary, than I can reckon the least part of that pleasure, which one that hath, and loves, an Orchard may find therein.'

THAT AVOWAL, made by William Lawson in his *A New Orchard and Garden*, which was published in 1618, may seem a little extreme to us today. Yet something of that old vision lingers, brought down to us by the prose and poetry of the past. The orchards of our imagination conform not to those of contemporary life with their bleak, uniform rows of dwarf trees, but to the romantic ideal of older fashions: places of fragrance, blossom and birdsong in which grow many species and varieties of fruit tree.

It seems likely that the word 'orchard' was derived from the Latin *hortus*, a garden (which in late Latin became *ortus* or *orto*), combined with 'yard'. Certainly in the ninth century the word *ortyeard* was in existence, written in Middle English variously as *orch-yard*, *ortyard* and *orchard*. As time passed the meaning of the word changed too. Originally an enclosed piece of land used for horticulture generally, it came to be a garden for herbs and fruit trees, and finally just for fruit trees. In 1845 it was defined in *The Florist's Journal* as 'Orchards: portions of ground appropriated to the growth of fruit trees only'.

There were certainly orchards and fruit gardens in England during the Roman occupation, and probably — although there is no direct evidence — some cultivation of fruit even before that. Information about the earliest interest in fruit is hard-won from archaeology and paleobotany. Even in medieval times evidence about orchards is sketchy, gained from incidental references in manuscript sources: household accounts, poems, treatises, translations, plans and illuminated manuscripts and books. From such material we perceive that fruit gardening was actively pursued, although we do not know the precise pattern of how an early medieval garden in England was planted and worked. The picture is clearer from the sixteenth century onwards, when gardening books began to be written and printed.

There were, however, two medieval works of immense popularity all over Europe which had a considerable influence upon contemporary garden planning and on later thinking. One was *Opus Ruralium Commodorum* by Petrus de Crescentiis, which contained a section describing gardens of herbs, gardens for men of moderate means, and gardens for kings and other rich lords. This book is based on the work of Roman writers such as Varro, Cato and Columella, their ideas being adapted to medieval taste. Crescentiis describes lawns, delightful turf seats, hedges of fruit or nut trees, and walks and bowers planted with fruit trees. All these features are to be found in later medieval gardens as described in literature and depicted in paintings.

Another greatly influential work was the *Romaunt of the Rose*, written by Guillaume de Lorris and Jean de Meung at the end of the thirteenth century, and popular for a good two hundred years. Inside the walled garden of the *Romaunt* there are wonderful trees, flowers and herbs. Among the trees are 'strange nut trees', nutmegs and cinnamon, but there are also many more familiar, or as Chaucer translates it, 'hoomly' trees.

> *And many hoomly trees ther were,*
> *That peaches, coynes and apples, bere.*
> *Medlars, ploumes, peres, chesteynes,*
> *Cheryse, of which many on fayne is,*
> *Notes, aleys, and bolas*
> *That for to seen it was solas . . .*

(Coynes = quinces; chesteynes = chestnuts; notes = nuts; many on fayne is = many a one is fond; aleys = serviceberries; bolas = bullaces.)

Chaucer's version of this poem is almost identical in its fruits with the original, so it should not be taken literally as an account of an English orchard; that said, however, it is likely that all of the 'hoomly' fruits, at least, were familiar to his readers. The line on cherries is his own, tempting us to think that he himself was among the many with a taste for them, and that perhaps even as early as the fourteenth century they were a speciality of his home county, Kent.

If we try to look back further into the English past and discern what early Anglo-Saxons would expect to grow in their 'wort yards' or 'plant gardens', we shall find no evidence; but there is a valuable record from the continent in the shape of a plan of the Benedictine monastery of St Gall, dating from about 820. The monastery, named after an Irish monk who travelled with St Columba's mission to Europe in the early seventh century, had been established for about a hundred years when the plan was drawn. It shows a large, self-sufficient community with many specialized buildings, a farm, a kitchen garden, a physic garden and an orchard which is also a cemetery. In the orchards there are plots marked specifically for apples, pears, plums, service trees, quinces, almonds, hazelnuts, walnuts, chestnuts, bay trees, peaches, mulberries and figs.

The Rule of St Benedict encouraged religious houses to be self-sufficient and gave great importance to manual labour: according to Benedict, '*Qui orat et laborat cor levat ad Deus cum manibus*' (he who prays and works lifts his heart up to God in his hands). It is probable that monasteries in England at that period also had gardens and orchards. Certainly they feature in a plan of Canterbury Cathedral and monastery of about 1165, and also in an early plan of Bicester Priory and in many other monastic documents. A Papal Bull of Alexander III in 1176 confiscated the property of the monks of Winchenley in Gloucestershire, 'with the town of Swiring and all its orchards', and twelfth-century Llanthony Priory in the Honddu valley acquired an orchard of twelve acres during the reign of King John. That the horticultural activities of the religious houses were widespread and profitable can also be deduced from the fact that in 1305 Edward I thought it worthwhile to impose a tithe on their fruits and garden produce.

Lay gardens were laid out in the same style as monastic ones, sometimes within the walls of castles, sometimes – more vulnerably – outside them. There is a description of how fruit trees outside the city walls were destroyed during the seige of Carlisle. No doubt un-settled times often made for problems in orchard maintenance. Traces of the existence of what must have been considerable gardens and orchards come to the surface here and there throughout the early Exchequer and Pipe rolls. There are payments to the orchard-men of King Henry II; of the cost of vineyard maintenance in the time of Edward I; and receipts from the sale of fruit from the gardens at Windsor. A specific account for the year 1295–96 shows that the Earl of Lincoln's garden in Holborn produced large quantities of grapes, apples, pears, cherries and nuts.

The picture we get is bound to be somewhat distorted because the records most likely to be carefully kept and long preserved are those relating to the households of royalty, the nobility and rich monasteries. It is certain, however, that gardens and orchards were also kept by people of less elevated status. Gardeners employed by London citizens, as well as those of barons, earls and bishops, were in the custom of selling their surplus fruit and vegetables near a side gate of St Paul's churchyard. By 1345 this market had become an annoyance to the monks of nearby St Austin, who petitioned the mayor and aldermen for its removal. The gardeners counter-petitioned and the matter was finally settled by moving the market to the back of St Austin's churchyard, which incommoded the monks less.

By the early fourteenth century the cultivation of fruit was clearly well understood and turned to profit, and some of the produce was available at all levels of society, not only to the knightly company portrayed in Chaucer's *Romaunt*. The Reeve in *Canterbury Tales*, for example, speaks of medlars with familiar knowledge; and Langland describes the poor bringing fruit and vegetables to Piers Plowman:

Alle the pore peple pescodden fetten,
Benes and baken apples thei brought in her lappes,
Chibolles and chervelles and ripe chiries manye.

(fetten = fetch; her = their; chibolles = onions.)

Later in this poem we hear of plum and pear trees being torn up by their roots during a terrible storm which to judge by its more than ordinary ferocity was the one recorded by several chroniclers in 1362.

The same wide range of fruits grown in the monastery gardens and mentioned by Chaucer and Langland was being sold in the London markets and hawked through the city's streets in the seventeenth century. At about this time composers began to be attracted by the songs and cries of street sellers. William Weelkes, Orlando Gibbon and Richard Dering, in particular, worked the songs of these traders into compositions of great interest and robust beauty.

They were often written as part songs for several voices, contriving an eccentric but very exciting sound. The first I ever heard was by Weelkes, and I remember the surprising first impression of the clear cries with the sudden changes in tune and the ringing language. It was only later that I discovered these tunes to be those of the original street cries that were sung over centuries in the streets of London. As late as 1711 Addison was writing that 'people know the wares ... rather by their Tunes than by their words; insomuch that I have sometimes seen a Country Boy run out to buy Apples of a Bellows-mender, and Gingerbread from a Grinder of Knives and Scissors.'

In Weelkes's *Street Cries* the fruits come after a fine litany of fish:

> Quick periwinkles; hot apple pies; hot pudding pies; hot pippin pies;
> Apples fine, pears fine, medlars fine, cherry ripe;
> Ripe strawberry ripe, fine Seville oranges; fine lemons;
> Fine pomegranates; ripe chestnuts; ripe walnuts ...

Eighteen kinds of fruit, some imported, many home-grown, occur in the various versions of the London cries. Some of them, such as 'Hott baked Wardens, hott' and 'Roasted pippins piping hot' were sold cooked. In the fourteenth-century *Piers Plowman* there are kitchen boys calling 'Hot pies', and in an eighteenth-century poem tempting 'Diddle diddle dumplins, hot ... with walnuts nice and brown' is one of the cries.

By the seventeenth century it is no longer necessary to piece together information. It is there for us in books by writers such as William Lawson, John Parkinson, Sir Hugh Platt, John Evelyn, Ralph Austen and Leonard Meager: books which remain among the finest literature on fruits and flowers. These authors combined a high degree of practical skill with a subtle appreciation of both the sensual and the contemplative pleasures of an orchard. For them the orchard was not only of practical value but also a pleasure garden, a place of beauty and peace which offered relaxation and solace; and this image recurs in poetry, painting and the theatre.

'We will go walk a little in the orchard, And then to dinner', suggests Baptista in *The Taming of the Shrew*, requiring calm after the double assault on his nerves of a violent scene between his daughters and Petruchio's abrupt initiation of marriage negotiations. In *A*

Treatise of Fruit Trees Ralph Austen devotes a whole chapter to describing 'The Pleasures of an Orchard' and finds separate delights to rejoice each one of the five senses. There are the 'soft and gentle sounds' caused by the movement of boughs and leaves, and the 'sweet notes . . . of singing birds'; the feel of the 'coole fruits' and the 'refreshing ayres' to be found in the shaded walks, seats and arbours; the pleasing sight of the 'order of planting of the trees, their decent forms, the well compos'd allies' and 'the pleasant and delicate colours of the leaves, blossomes, and fruits, that shew themselves in great variety'; the 'most precious odour' of blossom 'perfuming the ayre throughout all the orchard'; and lastly the taste 'from all sorts of ripe and raw fruits, besides meats and drinks and many dainties made of them'.

It was in the famous green shade of such a place that Andrew Marvell found 'fair quiet' for meditation and was enraptured by the 'delicious solitude' among the trees. He was one of countless poets – Shakespeare, Herrick, Jonson, Lovelace and Suckling among them – who drew on the wealth of symbolism to be found in fruit. In the seventeenth century, as in no other, we find particular species and varieties named in poetic conceits and metaphors.

In life, as in literature, the symbolic value of fruit was considerable. The possession of orchards, fruit-tree arbours and espaliered walls became part of the self-image of a nobleman or gentleman, as we can see from their frequent appearance in the country-house paintings of the time. Can they all have been so perfectly beautiful as they are depicted? It is certain that they were not; the artists were not making a faithful imitation of reality but creating a picture of a way of life. And as artists and writers drew from life, and at times idealized it, they influenced fashions in gardening. Many makers of gardens must have worked with Francis Bacon's *Essay on Gardens* (1625) in mind.

This work evokes a garden of princely proportions, with 'fair alleys, ranged on both sides with fruit trees; and some pretty tufts of fruit trees, and arbours with seats.' Its walls were espaliered, and the varieties of fruit growing in it were many. Among the apples, two varieties are named: 'Ginnitings and Quadlins' (better known as Jenetings and Codlins). There were also cherries, plums, 'dammasins', and pears (the famous 'Wardon' among them), as well as strawberries, currants, raspberries and gooseberries. Some of the fruit grown in that ideal garden is less familiar to us today: medlars, 'bullises', quinces. Others strike us as exotic plants to find in English soil: figs, melocotones, nectarines, grape-vines, peaches, almonds. Others again required considerable gardening skill and intensive care: citrus fruits, for example, were to be found only in the richest gardens.

Bacon's garden is too grand to serve as inspiration to most present-day fruit growers, but there are many ways in which we would do better to look to the past rather than to modern enterprise. The gardeners of the past, like the private gardener of today, designed and planted for pleasure as well as for profit, and they have left us glimpses in both pictures and words of some of the most beautiful fruit gardens, by no means always on a grand scale, that ever existed in the western world. In those gardens they grew many varieties of fruit that we have lost or are in danger of losing, but which we can recover if we are prepared to grow them ourselves. If we follow the measures of the early gardeners, we may recall not only the fine flavours of historic and almost forgotten fruits but also the pleasures of the orchardists of the past.

CHAPTER TWO

Forgotten Fruits

ONLY A FEW out of the huge range of long-established fruits and fruit varieties are now available to us in the shops. Certain fruits have completely passed out of general use, among them medlars, quinces, chequers (the fruit of the wild service) and aleys *(Sorbus domestica)*. There are, however, nurseries which still hold stock of these fruit trees, sometimes in more than one variety. For a minimal outlay and effort, anyone with a garden can grow fruits of a kind it would be difficult and sometimes impossible to obtain in any other way. In addition to the pleasure of growing and eating the fruits, there is extra satisfaction in the knowledge that even a few unusual fruit trees in a small garden contribute to the bulwark against the trend towards standardization and blandness of taste in commercial production. Any garden anywhere can be a rare fruits reserve.

Medlars

In the mid-sixteenth century the botanist William Turner observed that medlar trees were common in England. Nowadays one has to search well to find them. The fruit resembles a small russet apple, with a thick skin which is rough and greenish-brown by the time it falls from the tree. The medlar is considerably more deeply indented than an apple at the end opposite the stalk. Turner gives 'open-ars tree' as an alternative name for it, and the fruits are still known as 'openers' in some parts of the country – this is the name for them used by Chaucer's Reeve. Another descriptive vernacular name from them, a politer one, comes from Scotland: 'how doup' or 'hose doup', meaning 'hollow berry'. The hollow is fringed with long dark ribbons, the remains of the flower-sepals.

The fruit falls from the tree in mid-November, but is still wood-hard and not fit to eat, unless you wish to follow the old herbalists' prescription for binding the bowel. Medlars must be left to become over-ripe, the natural process of decay being called, in this case, 'bletting'. When fully bletted they may, as John Parkinson wrote, 'be eaten by them who have no need of binding, and but onely for the pleasant sweetness of them when they are made mellow.' Left to themselves, medlars become bletted after a few sharp frosts, but as animals and birds also enjoy them, it is wise to gather your medlars when they are on the point of falling, and to store them wrapped in paper (or in straw, or bran) until they are properly extra-ripe.

Parkinson gives two kinds of English medlar, and a Neapolitan variety. There are also three varieties available today. One of these, the Nottingham (also known as the common medlar) is very old, and may be the same as Parkinson's 'lesser English medlar'. The Nottingham is believed to have been one of the first cultivated varieties, and is justly esteemed for its flavour. It is a small tree which can be relied upon to produce a rich crop of fruit.

Another old variety still available is the Dutch, which is also called the Great Dutch and the Monstrous. As these alternative names suggest, it is larger than the Nottingham in all its details. It was mentioned by John Evelyn in his *Gardener's Almanac* (1664) and was known to Duhamel in 1760. It tends to a weeping habit of growth and its fruit is well-flavoured, but it is a less substantial cropper than the Nottingham. The Royal Medlar, introduced by Rivers in 1860, has characteristics mid-way between the other two.

Medlars do not suit all palates, but the literary critic George Saintsbury who also wrote a classic book on wines, *Notes on a Cellar-book*, declared that 'the one fruit which seems to me to go best with *all* wine, from hock to sherry and from claret to port, is the medlar – an admirable and distinguished thing in itself, and a worthy mate for the best of liquors.' Its slightly rasping, granular texture (a characteristic of bletted fruits) and its lingering, slightly sweet, slightly winy flavour, makes the medlar seem like a natural comfit. Parkinson tells us that they were sometimes kept simply 'as a dish of ripe fruit at their fit season, to be served with other sorts to the table', and this seems as good a way as any to enjoy them. Alternatively the flesh can be spooned out of the tough skins and served with cream. Medlars roasted with butter and cloves are a traditional winter desert, and jelly or cheese made from them is recommended as an accompaniment to game.

The trees, particularly the Nottingham, are suitable for gardens of small or moderate size. They blossom in midsummer and the white flowers, set singly on the branch, make a delicate effect against the soft oval leaves. The larger flower of the Dutch is compared by the Rivers' nursery to that of a wild rose. The practice of grafting medlars onto whitethorn stock, mentioned by John Gerard in his *Herball* (1597), is still continued. The hardy, self-fertile trees grow slowly, but they are worth waiting for. A three-year-old Nottingham on thorn stock can produce a good crop of fruit.

Quinces

Soon after I began this book, a good friend brought me a basketful of quinces which he had found at the rather special fruit stall in Selborne which sells many unusual varieties of fruit. Though it was a cold and frosty day, he was compelled to drive all the way from Hampshire to Hertfordshire with the car-window open, or he would have been overwhelmed by the rich spicy smell of my quinces. This is so strong that it is always recommended that quinces be stored separately from any other fruit.

The true quince, *Cydonia oblonga* (not to be confused with the oriental quince, the species *Chaenomeles*), came originally from South-west Asia but has been cultivated in Europe for many centuries. John Parkinson, in 1629, gave a description which is still as good as any of the true quince.

> The Quince tree groweth oftentimes, to the height and bignesse of a good Apple tree, but more usually lower, with crooked and spreading armes and branches farre abroad, the leaves are somewhat round, and like the leaves of the Apple tree, but thicker, harder, fuller of veines, and white on the underside: the blossomes or flowers are white, now and then dasht over with blush, being large and open, like unto a single Rose: the fruit followeth, which when it is ripe is yellow, and covered with a white cotton or freeze, which in the younger is thicker and more plentifull, but waxeth lesse and lesse, as the fruit ripeneth, being bunched out many times in severall places, and round especially about the head, some greater, others smaller, some round like an Apple, others long like a Peare, of a strong heady sent . . .

Parkinson goes on to enumerate six varieties of quince, including the English Apple Quince, the Barbary Quince, the Brunswick

Medlar

Quince

Service Tree

Wild Service
Tree

Quince and the Portingall Peare Quince. His choice of the last three was endorsed by John Evelyn in his list – 'Quinces: the best'. As late as the mid-1920s the Apple-shaped Quince is to be found in fruit books, one manual describing it as 'one of the oldest varieties and still one of the best for all round purposes'; but sadly, I can find no fruit nursery which stocks it nowadays. Many nurseries, how-ever, do sell the Portugal, which was imported by John Tradescant in 1611 for Lord Burleigh and is still recommended as one of the best culinary quinces. The fruit, almost orange in colour when ripe, is large and pear-shaped and distinctly knobbed about the eye.

The quince was highly regarded in the seventeenth century. The oft-quoted Sir Thomas Browne wrote of 'the stomach's comforter, the pleasing Quince', and from Parkinson, there is high praise: 'There is no fruit growing in this Land that is of so many excellent uses as this, serving as well to make many dishes of meate for the table, as for banquets, and much more for the Physicall vertues . . .' He describes how they may be baked, pickled and made into con-serves, and mentions quince candy or 'condimacke'. This sweetmeat is rendered as 'cotiniate' by Gerard (it is known as 'cotignac' in France) and is almost identical with the 'quince comfit' of an eighteenth-century recipe. It was the end to which I put my gift quinces; and as it improves with keeping, I set it aside for Christmas, thinking our stomachs might then well be in need of soothing.

Quinces make some of the best jam in the world if you prefer a preserve of some sharpness and character to the excessively sweet jams that most dessert fruit makes. 'Chare de Quyinces' is men-tioned in John Russell's *Boke of Nurture* of 1460 among many other table delicacies. A slice of quince added to an apple dish gives an interestingly spicy flavour. Both these uses were known by the Romans, who also had a recipe which they called *melomeli*. Colu-mella's version of this entails placing the fruits in a wide-necked flagon, covering them with willow twigs and filling the vessel with honey. Another use is suggested in passing in Shakespeare's *Romeo and Juliet*. As the Capulet household is busy with the preparations for the ill-fated feast which is to celebrate the marriage of Juliet to Paris, the nurse informs Lady Capulet that 'They call for dates and quinces in the pastry'. It was, in fact, a tradition deriving from the Romans that quinces should be served at weddings since they were seen as tokens of love.

William Lawson grew quinces as far north as Yorkshire, though he was more than a little doubtful about recommending this. 'We meddle not with Apricots nor Peaches nor scarcely with Quinces, which will not like our cold parts, unless they be helped with some reflex of the Sun.' Accordingly he advised that quinces, which are small trees, should be planted at the south side or end of the orchard, where they would receive the most sun without shading other trees. The 'blush pink' flowers of quince have recommended themselves to gardeners to the extent that nowadays many quince trees are retained in gardens only for the beauty of their blossom. The Japanese quince *(Chaenomeles japonica)* is grown specifically for its flowers, and at least one nursery notes in its current catalogue that the true quince has 'fine flowers' and 'could be grown as an ornamental tree'. Certainly in the past, quinces were grown both for beauty and usefulness. They were generally planted where people would pass by and enjoy them. John Aubrey's sketch for Deepdene shows quinces planned along a walk near to the house, and the Parliamentary survey made in 1649 of the extensive gardens at Wimbledon designed for Henrietta Maria describes how 'In the inside of the fourth outward walk or alley are sixteen quince trees, well planted and ordered.'

As with many of the rarer fruits, some modern nurseries catalogue quince without stating the variety, so it is as well to enquire further to make sure of getting the variety you want. The Portugal is sold in several places and it is also possible to find another old variety, the Pear-shaped quince. The type known as Vranja (or sometimes Bereczki after the Hungarian pomologist) is imported from the Balkans where it has long been grown. Other good but more recent varieties are Champion and Meech's Prolific, both from America and popular at the turn of this century.

Quinces are self-fertile so you can happily plant a single tree. They like a moist situation, warmth and a deep, rich soil without too much lime. Under these conditions they can start producing fruit at five to six years old. Quinces are sold as bushes, standards and half standards and can be grown, as in Parkinson's day, against a wall. Lawrence Hills suggests that instead of buying an expensive wall-trained quince, you can train a bush quince to a wall by snipping off the outward-growing branches at sideways-pointing buds. Quinces also grow well among apples as standard trees in an orchard.

The Service Family

Old gardens are the only places where you may come unexpectedly across a quince tree. Medlars can occasionally be discovered planted or naturalised in ancient hedges. There is, however, nothing to compare with the excitement of coming across wild service trees deep in an old wood.

Wild Service is native to Britain and it is named in at least one Anglo-Saxon charter. It is mostly a tree of southern woodlands, though a recent survey showed it to grow wild as far north as Westmorland, and in gardens much further north. I consider the leaves of the Wild Service to be among the most beautiful of all our forest trees. They are palmate and shining like those of a plane tree, but the middle part of the leaf is elongated like that of a Field Maple. The autumn shades are as rich as any maple's.

The little fruits, which turn brown with the November frosts as the leaves go crimson, are eaten bletted. I happen to like the slightly sweet taste and nutty texture of service berries but in past times they were recommended more for their medicinal value than their palatability (though John Evelyn enjoyed them). Service berries, like medlars, are binding: in Parkinson's words they are 'fit to be taken of them that have any scouring or laske' though he warns direly 'take heed, lest if you bind too much, more pain and danger may come thereof then of the scouring.' (I must add that I never felt any ill effects from eating service berries.)

A mid-nineteenth century Flora says that bunches of wild service berries, or chequers as they were usually called in the south, were sold in shops, mainly to children, who saw them perhaps as natural sweets. They were still to be found in Kentish shops in the early years of this century. Now, however, few people know how they taste: a tradition in fruit which probably went back beyond Anglo-Saxon times into pre-history, has been broken.

Another *Sorbus* species is the sorb apple *(Sorbus domestica)*, which was much planted in medieval and Tudor orchards. There are two forms in cultivation, apple-shaped *(maliformis)* and pear-shaped *(pyriformis)*. I have tried only *maliformis*, which has a delicious winey taste. There is one of each kind in the Oxford Botanic Gardens but outside of special collections, they are extremely rare. Only one example of the sorb apple has ever been found growing in wild conditions in Britain: a mysterious solitary tree in the middle of the Wyre Forest. This has given rise to intense speculation about whether *Sorbus domestica* can be considered a native species. That old tree, known as the Whitty Pear of Wyre, died in 1862 but cuttings and suckers from it were planted in many parks and gardens where they have thrived. A direct descendant of the Wyre original was replanted in the same spot as its ancestor in 1913. This tree thrived until recently, when it was blown down in a gale, but the stump is suckering thickly.

There are a great number of *Sorbus* species and hybrids. Whitebeams too have edible fruits and the Forest of Dean has at least three species of whitebeam and a number of hybrids including a cross between the common whitebeam and wild service. This usually appears in books as the service tree of Fontainebleau after the woods where it was found in the early part of the eighteenth century, but I have also seen it called the Cornish whitebeam. The fruits resemble large white cherries.

Another whitebeam hybrid of south-west Britain is *Sorbus devoniensis*, known locally as French hales. It produces tasty fruits which used to find their way into Devon shops. There is one nursery which still sells this tree. Appropriately, it is in Devon.

Apart from the common whitebeam and the rowan, the old-fashioned *Sorbus* species are very difficult to obtain. If you come across some wild service berries, you may succeed in growing from seed, but I know of only one nursery where you can buy stock of it or of *Sorbus domestica*.

Mulberry

William Forsyth wrote of mulberries at the beginning of the nineteenth century that the older the tree, the better the fruit, but added 'I am sorry to say that this pleasant and valuable fruit is but little cultivated in this country'. It is still a rare tree, but there are some very old specimens which bear out Forsyth's adage and produce excellent mulberries. Some of these, such as the one in Charlton Park, are believed to date back to James I, who instigated a wave of mulberry tree planting in an effort to increase the silk industry in Britain. There were, however, mulberries growing 'in diverse gardens in England' at least fifty years before James' accession, as

William Turner recorded in his *Names of Herbes* (1548). Thomas Tusser, Gerard and John Parkinson also describe the varieties of mulberry and their culture. Gerard notes that of all the trees in the orchard, the mulberry is the last to bloom, a feature observed also by Barnaby Googe, the Elizabethan poet: 'when soever you see the Mulberie begin to spring, you may be sure that winter is at an end.' For this reason the ancients called the mulberry the wisest tree and devoted it to Minerva, but Henry Hawkins in his beautiful emblem book *Parthenia Sacra* (1633) wrote of 'the Mulberrie of Patience'.

Parkinson commended the 'sweete and pleasant' taste of the mulberry when it was 'full ripe' but warns that 'the juice whereof is so red, that it will stain the hands of them that handle and eate them,' a fact alluded to twice by Shakespeare and experienced by every mulberry gatherer. The white mulberry is the tree which silk moths are said to prefer but the common or large black mulberry *(Morus nigra)* is the one grown for its fruits, and is available from a number of nurseries. The mulberry is an attractive spreading tree, an asset for an orchard or good-sized garden, and it can also be wall trained, a procedure recommended for colder parts. Most of us have sung the children's ring game 'Here we go round the mulberry bush' or the haunting nineteenth-century song 'As the dew flies over the mulberry tree', but few of us are familiar with the tree or its fruits. It would be pleasant to see the characteristic zig-zag branches and broad dark green leaves growing over more garden walls, to be enjoyed in centuries to come.

CHAPTER THREE

Exotic Fruits
in English Gardens

Against the South wall are one Apricocke from Mr Rea, three Apricockes from London, one peache from a French stone, raised at Bettisfield 1660 and two red-heart cherries from Trevallyn. In the corner next to the turf walk one pear from Bowen, I think a bergamot.

Against the stack of chimneys and the wall between the chimney and the door are a rare vine, a vine from K. Eyton, a Bon Chretien pear and a peach from a French stone raised at Bettisfield 1660.

Against the wall by the green turf walk are peaches that were removed from Haulton which came thither from London and one peach raised at Bettisfield from a French stone 1660, which peach is next to the Great Garden door next the orchard; there are also 2 heart cherries and a cornelian tree at the end by the yew tree.

Against the wall by the gravelly walk towards the highway are all peaches, two of which viz. the first next to the Court Gate is a Roman peach and the third from the gate is a nutmeg peach; the next are all peaches from stones set by me at Lewisham and removed thence to Bettisfield.

In the little court with the stone stairs against the little garden wall are three peaches from Mr. Bate viz. a Morillopeach next the little Garden Door, then a Newington peach and then a Persian peach. Against the other wall, over against these peaches are two plums from Rea. In the little garden against the south wall, beginning from the house, are four common apricockes then an early apricocke then a bellowes peach near the corner. Against the east wall of the little garden by the two sycamores are, beginning from the south wall, first three peaches raised 1660 at Bettisfield from French stones, then a peach de Pau, then a Savoy peach.

THIS EXTRACT from a memorandum written by Sir Thomas Hanmer recording the fruits trees in the Great Garden at Bettisfield conveys something of the energy which was devoted to fruit gardening in the latter half of the seventeenth century. It also shows the enterprise which went into the cultivation of a range and variety of species which we would now regard almost exclusively as exotics and expect to buy from shops rather than raise them ourselves. As well as his *Garden Book*, written by 1659 but not published until this century, there were among Sir Thomas Hanmer's papers a number of other gardening notes, including a piece entitled 'Of Vines', which contains some sound advice on the taking of cuttings, and a supplementary essay which describes 'Colonell Blunt's Vineyard'. There is also an account 'Of Fruite Trees and Orchards' in which he writes about peaches, apricots, nectarines and vines as naturally as he does about apples, pears, plums and cherries.

Some of the records compiled by Sir Thomas Hanmer of the plants which he bought from nurseries, both English and French, have also survived the centuries. One such list of plants, sent by George Ricketts of Hogsden, itemizes by name no less than twenty-one varieties of peach and nectarine as well as an interesting range of cherries, pears and apples and the July flowers (or gilly flowers) which he obtained from this supplier in 1667.

We know from his papers that Sir Thomas also experimented with growing his own fruit trees from stones and that other stock in his garden and orchard was given him by friends. John Rea, who gave him, among other things, 'three Apricots, a cornelian cherry and a Turkey plum' was the author of the highly influential *Flora, Ceres and Pomona*. The dedicatory letter which prefaces this book affirms that Sir Thomas Hanmer and his garden were its inspiration and that the author gratefully acknowledges the 'happy Aquaintance' which 'reanimated my drooping endevours . . . and the free Bounty [which] furnished me with many noble and new varieties'.

John Evelyn, author of *Sylva*, *Pomona* and the *Gardening Almanac*, was also a friend of Sir Thomas Hanmer. Hanmer, Rea and Evelyn were Royalists, as were other famous gardeners of the time such as Arthur Capel, Earl of Essex (patron of Moses Cook) and his brother Henry Capel, Baron of Tewkesbury, but gardening transcended politics; the Cromwellian general Lord Lambert, who was also a tulip enthusiast was proud to have in his collection a tulip, the Agate Hanmer, which Sir Thomas Hanmer had introduced to England. A benefit of the uncertain political climate of the late seventeenth century was that it forced men of both loyalties into periods of retirement on their country estates where they devoted considerable vigour and intelligence to their gardening pursuits. General Fairfax's withdrawal into private life on his estate at Nun Appleton was shared for a while by Andrew Marvell and it is believed that the most famous poem about a garden in the English language had its inspiration in this Yorkshire estate. If this is so, it is worth noting that even so far north, the garden contained not only 'ripe Apples' but 'the luscious clusters of the vine', 'the nectarene' and 'curious peach'.

Seventeenth-century gardeners used every skill to help on the fruit trees accustomed to warmer southern climates and with such care and tenderness, the plants thrived and fruited. The preferences and requirements of each species were carefully remarked. Some varieties were more responsive than others and this too was heeded. Much of what we know today about growing such fruit as peaches, apricots, nectarines, almonds and walnuts is a direct legacy from four centuries ago. The varieties cherished by these early experts were selected so wisely that some of them are still recommended today.

Citrus Cultivation

The cultivation of some of the more tender species was a specialist activity, and remains so today. Only a very few enthusiasts now try seriously to raise citrus fruits in Britain. The requirements for the successful culture of orange trees were known in the beginning of the seventeenth century but they were expensive and intensive of labour, though as John Parkinson wrote, 'with some extraordinary looking and tending of it' the orange could be coaxed into fruit.

> If therefore any be desirous to keepe this tree, he must so provide for it, that it be preserved from any cold, either in the winter or spring, and exposed to the comfort of the sun in summer. And for that purpose some keep them in great square boxes, and lift them to and fro by iron hooks on the sides, or cause them to be rowled by trundles, or small wheels under them, to place them in an house or close gallerie for the winter time: others plant them against a brick wall in the ground, and defend them by a shed of boardes, covered over with seare-cloth in the winter, and by the warmth of a stove . . . give them some comfort in the colder times: but no tent or meane provision will preserve them.

One of the grandest of the early orangeries was that of Queen

Henrietta Maria at Wimbledon, where a sunken garden had been converted into an orange garden. It is the first item described in the parliamentary survey of 1649. In the elegant 'Garden House' (one of the first greenhouses specifically designed for the purpose of sheltering plants) were 'forty-two Oringe trees' standing just as Parkinson prescribes in square boxes, and bearing 'fair and large oringes'. There were also eighteen other orange trees which had not yet come into fruit, and two great rarities, a fruit-bearing lemon tree and a pomecitron. We know exactly how it looked because an engraving by Henry Winstanley of the garden front of Wimbledon Palace, including the orangery, still survives.

Such gardens were and remained the prerogative of the very rich, though as the century progressed, orangeries came more into fashion. Pepys visited Lord Brooke's garden in Hackney in 1666 and 'here I first saw oranges grow, some green, some half, some a quarter, some full ripe on the same tree . . . I pulled off a little one by stealth (the man being mightily curious of them) and eat it, and it was just as other little green oranges are – as big as half the end of my little finger'. Orange trees were still a curiosity at the end of the century, when Celia Fiennes visited a country house in Wiltshire and exclaimed at 'the first oring trees I ever saw'. A beautiful representation survives of the orange tree garden at Chiswick, painted by Rysbrack in about 1730. By this date there were also stately orangeries at Hampton Court and Kensington Palace, and later at Kew. They had become something of a status symbol for the mighty.

The Famous Pineapple

The most famous painting of a single fruit is that of *John Rose presenting a Pineapple to Charles II*. In fact, Horace Walpole made the first recorded reference to the picture under this title as late as 1780, and there have been subsequent doubts about whether this was, as the story had it, the first pineapple grown in England (pineapple culture was imperfectly understood), whether the scene is English (the grand house and garden in the background seems not to be), and even whether the kneeling character is John Rose the royal gardener. Whatever the truth may be, the fact remains that the presentation of this rare fruit to the King was thought a significant enough event to occasion a grand painting. A home-grown pineapple at this time would have been a great rarity, as in fact, it still is.

Apricots

One of the favourites among the 'outlandish' fruits was the apricot, probably introduced from Italy in about 1542 by John Woolf, gardener to Henry VIII. In his *Names of Herbes* (1548) William Turner devoted a section to apricots:

> *Malus armeniaca* . . . some englishe me [may] call the fruite an Abricok. Me thynke seinge that we have very fewe of these trees as yet, it were better to cal it, an hasty Peche tree because it is lyke a pech and it is a great whyle rype before the pech trees . . .

Turner's suggestion is actually an anglicization of the name 'apricot' itself, which, coming to us through the Portuguese *albricoque* or Old Spanish *albarcoque*, is derived from the Latin *praecox*, 'early ripe'.

There is a considerable amount of later evidence that within a few decades of their introduction apricots were widely grown. Tusser, in 1573, includes 'apricocks' in his list of fruits to be set in the month of January. Gerard noted 'These trees do grow in my garden, and now adaies in many other gentlemans gardens throughout all England'. From Shakespeare's references we can gather that apricots fruited well and that their flavour was highly esteemed. There were 'apricocks and dewberries' among the delectable fruits that the queen of the fairies ordered for her lover. Though the reference is anachronistic, since it is unlikely that apricots were grown in England in the late fourteenth century, Shakespeare uses an accurate description of their cultivation to provide an extended metaphor in *Richard III*:

> *Go bind thou up those dangling apricocks,*
> *Which like unruly children make their sire*
> *Stoop with oppression of their prodigal weight.*
> *Give some supportance to the bending twigs.*
> *Go thou, and like an executioner*
> *Cut off the heads of too fast growing sprays . . .*

There is a nice apricot allusion in Ben Jonson's *Every Man in his Humour* (1598) (in which Shakespeare is known to have acted).

Edward Knowall's father, who is excessively solicitous for his son's morals, is likened to an over-zealous gardener by another character, Wellbred, who writes to young Edward 'Leave thy vigilant father alone to number over his green apricots evening and morning.'

Hogg (in his *Fruit Manual* of 1862), described no less than twenty-seven varieties of apricot which would fruit in England. The earlier gardening books listed fewer; Parkinson had six, Evelyn four and Sir Thomas Hanmer four. Philip Miller, who had a special interest in apricots, described eight varieties including one, the Breda, which is still recommended in the Royal Horticultural Society's *Fruit Manual* today. Some of the others mentioned in these old lists, such as the Masculine, the Roman, the Brussells and the Turkey, were still grown into the late nineteenth century but have faded out since then. Of the older varieties which are still available, one which is as popular as ever for its rich sweet flavour, large fruits and reliable crop, is the Moorpark, a famous apricot which first fruited in 1760 in England, at Moor Park in Hertfordshire. It was brought over by Admiral Anson, who seems to have made time for this between pirating against the Spanish, circumnavigating the world and defeating the French off Cape Finisterre. An apricot called Hemskerk, whose origins are obscure, is recommended by Hogg in 1862 and also by the Royal Horticultural Society and Lawrence Hills. Just over a century old is Rivers' New Large Early, raised in 1873 and still valued for its fine flavour. An apricot now grown in America, although it seems to have gone out of favour here, is called Shipley after the Miss Shipley who raised it as a seedling at Blenheim, early in the nineteenth century, when her father was gardener to the Duke of Marlborough.

Apricots will fruit well out of doors over much of England, provided conditions are reasonably mild. They are self-fertile, though the artificial aid of brush pollination is often employed to ensure setting a crop. In the south it is possible to grow them as standard trees (as was done a century or more ago, according to gardening manuals) although they are grateful for the extra warmth of a wall and espaliers are generally more successful. In the north extra protection has to be given. In spite of William Lawson's advice to 'meddle not with apricots' in Yorkshire, there is today a nursery as far north as Aberdeen which sells both an apricot and a peach, recommending that the apricot should be grown out of doors on a frost-free wall, although the peach requires a cool greenhouse.

Peaches

Peaches are mentioned at least twice in Anglo-Saxon herbals. Since much of the substance of these old herbals was translated from classical sources, this cannot be taken as proof that the fruit was grown in Britain at that time; but it does at least show that Anglo-Saxon scribes, herbalists and monks knew of the existence of peaches and had a vernacular name for them. Pliny knew the peach as *'persica'*. It was also referred to as *Malus persica*, the name by which William Turner knew it and which he translated in 1548 as 'in English a peche'. The Romans may well have planted peaches in their English gardens, and a few may have been grown in monastery orchards, but it was not until the late sixteenth century that a real interest was taken in the peach and its varieties.

It was not only for their delicious fruits that the old gardeners loved apricots and peaches; their appreciation of the beauty of the flowers led them sometimes into a pleasant quandary as to where to plant them, as in this instance when John Parkinson deliberated on the subject of double-flowered peaches:

> The beautiful show of these . . . sorts of flowers hath made me to insert them into this garden in that for their worthiness I am unwilling to be without them, although the rest of their kindes I have transferred into the Orchard.

Thomas Johnson who was the editor of the 1631 edition of Gerard, and well acquainted with John Parkinson, also knew and liked this double-flowered peach although he says that, in his experience, the beautiful flowers only rarely developed into fruit. Johnson, Parkinson and after them John Evelyn all describe several varieties of peach of which one, the Newington, was still known by Doctor Hogg in 1862, though it appears to be available no more. According to Parkinson it was 'of excellent good relish . . . ripe about Bartholemew tide'. Hogg says it has a very vinous flavour, and indeed many of the older varieties seem to have had a rich, spicy, winey taste which was matched by names such as Nutmeg Peach, the Grand Carnation, the Queen's Peach and the Peach du Troy. Peaches can be very cheap in the shops in season nowadays, but it is hard to find much correspondence between some of these small, beigy, tasteless tennis ball peaches and the descriptions of rich fruits of the past. Fine, ripe peaches travel badly because they bruise easily, so the imported market varieties are selected for early picking and keeping qualities. This is why one never has a chance to taste the best-flavoured varieties, or even to try the commercial kinds at their sun-ripened best.

On John Evelyn's recommended list is also a variety known as Admirable, which was first recorded by Le Lectier in 1628 although it was grown in England only since about 1729. Some of the other species Evelyn mentions – Boudin, Mignon and Musque Violet – were known to Robert Hogg in the late nineteenth century but only the Admirable survived to the present century to be noted by Bunyard in 1925, and he comments that it was then only 'rarely grown'.

Of all the early varieties only the Bellegarde, known since 1732 (in France it was called Galande), is still obtainable, and from only one or two nurseries. This is a variety recommended by the Royal Horticultural Society, as is also the Peregrine, another richly flavoured and juicy peach introduced by that most famous of peach-growing nurseries, Rivers, at the beginning of this century. The Peregrine may be grown out of doors, in a sunny sheltered place, in mild climates, as a bush or a tree; but in the north most nurseries recommend growing it inside a greenhouse.

Nectarines

It may come as a surprise to learn that peaches and nectarines are not separate species but varieties of *Prunus persica*, the former downy-skinned, the latter smooth. At least one well-recommended nectarine, the Lord Napier, was grown from the stone of a peach, the early Albert; and the Peregrine peach was grown from a Spenser nectarine stone.

Parkinson considered the nectarine 'more firm than the peach, and more delectable in taste . . .' and he seems to have been regarded as the expert on these fruits. It was to Parkinson that Thomas Johnson referred the readers of the *Herball* for further information.

The 'Roman Red Nectorin' was recommended not only by these two writers, but also by John Evelyn and it was still grown in 1925 when Bunyard praised its 'rich musky flavour', remarking that 'for its vigour and firmness' it was 'quite worth preserving'. He referred of course to the fruits, and his words read ironically now that the variety itself is lost to us. Lost also are Evelyn's 'richly flavoured' Murrey and the Musque Violet known to Hogg as the Violette Hative which was reckoned by Bunyard to have been known in France since 1659. Even the one nectarine of ancient name which is still available, the Elruge, is believed not to be the original variety mentioned by Sir Thomas Hanmer, by Evelyn and by Miller and raised at a nursery near Spitalfields (it was an anagram on the name of the nurseryman, Gurle). The oldest nectarine readily available nowadays is the Pitmaston Orange which was introduced about 1815. (It was also known as Williams Orange and Williams Seedling since it was raised by Mr Williams of Pitmaston near Worcester.) It has yellow flesh and is commended for its fine rich sweet flavour. The Pitmaston Orange is recommended by the Royal Horticultural Society, as are two other nectarines still available from nurseries: the Lord Napier and the Pineapple. Both these last were raised by Rivers in the latter half of the nineteenth century, as were also the well-regarded Early Rivers and Humboldt. Of the Humboldt Bunyard remarks, like Parkinson four centuries before him, that it is a variety worth growing for the flowers alone. Lawrence Hills gives it pride of place for flavour and adds that it also has the practical advantage of blossoming later than the other peaches and therefore missing some of the frosts.

Like the peach, the slightly more tender nectarine will succeed in bush or standard form in the south of England, but is more reliable fan-trained against a wall. Nectarines are self fertile, but as with apricots the use of brush pollination is a wise precaution.

Figs

There is extreme difficulty nowadays in getting hold of any fig other than the Brown Turkey, although about fifty years ago one had a choice of sixteen or so varieties, and only a little over a century ago Hogg was exulting in no less than twenty-four different kinds. We know that figs were enjoyed as early as the reign of Edward I when it was recorded that a 'frail' (rush basket) full of figs was purchased from a Spanish ship, along with oranges, dates, pomegranates and citrons. We do not learn much about fig varieties from the writers of the sixteenth and seventeenth centuries. They mention between two and six kinds of fig, mostly described by shape and colour, and these do not correspond to the names in later use. However, Hogg correlates the blue fig mentioned by Evelyn with the Brown Turkey fig. Ralph Austen wrote of this variety 'I know of but one kind of Figs that come to ripeness with us: the great Blew-fig, as large as a Catherine Pear. The trees grow in divers gardens in Oxford, set against a south wall, and be spread up with nayles and Leathers.' Philip Miller of the *Gardeners Dictionary* was particularly interested in fig culture and described eighteen varieties, some of them new to Britain.

Fig trees, with their beautiful great leaves, were popular in gardens and did especially well in those near the sea, although they can certainly thrive away from the coast as well. I once shared a house on Primrose Hill where there was a fig tree against a wall which produced fruit every year with no tending whatsoever, and there are fig trees by the National Gallery which also give fruit. A fruit manual of 1905 gives Worthing as the centre of British fig culture, a fact confirmed by a local nurseryman. Fresh ripe figs used to be sent from there to Covent Garden for sale, but now unfortunately the fig orchards have gone and the trade has ceased. By the beginning of the eighteenth century, when Thomas Fairchild published the *City Gardener*, London was already a polluted smoky place, but Fairchild specially mentions the good figs to be found there, in particular those in the Rolls garden of Chancery Lane and in Dr Bennet's garden in Cripplegate. In 1674 Captain Gurle, the nurseryman of Spitalfields, supplied white 'figges' at five shillings each and the 'great bleu figge' at two shillings. Fig trees were carried in a number of nursery catalogues in the seventeenth and eighteenth centuries in Bristol and London, and even as far north as York, where in 1775 the firm of John & George Telford sold fig trees at 9d each.

Although where I live in Hertfordshire is about as far from the sea as you can get in England, I am inclined to think that figs may have been grown here since one of the many names for Brown Turkey is Ashridge Forcing, perhaps taken from the Duke of Bridgewater's beautiful Ashridge estate and garden just across the valley (though the name seems to indicate that they were grown under glass rather than in the open).

Though figs are a sun-loving species, figs grown in England can taste good. Some varieties are very rewarding: the chocolate-skinned

Brown Turkey, rich, sweet and crimson within; the dull-brown Brunswick with its pink-tinged flesh; and the delicate White Marseilles, sweet and almost opalescent. William Turner (1548) knew the fig as a garden tree, and they were probably grown a good deal before that. It seems fairly certain that the 'wide branched sycamore' at Canterbury, under which Thomas à Becket's murderers are recorded to have thrown their cloaks, was a fig tree. I think there were true sycamores in Britain at the time (they are certainly represented in medieval churches) but it seems more likely that a large tree in monastery grounds, with an orchard adjacent, would be a fig. (Figs, such as the biblical fig of Zacharias, were often recorded as 'sycamores' because of the species *Ficus sycomorus*, the Sycamore fig, well known by the ancient herbalists.)

Grapevines

Winemaking is an activity which attracts mystique, whether it is practised on a grand or private scale. There are those who disparage anything but well-known French or German wines, but there are vines in small gardens and vineyards in the south of England and in Wales which produce more than passable wines, even in amateur hands. When the parents of my best friend moved to Thaxted in Essex, they found in their garden a large old vine. During their first year the grapes were abundant and Pauline produced a wine which has made her mildly famous in the neighbourhood: a light delicate dry white, of the kind for which the best English vineyards are again becoming renowned.

Although English wine is heavily taxed and expensive, the number of vineyards has increased greatly in the last decade, standing now at over five hundred, more than at any time since the Middle Ages. It is part of a long tradition: in the third century, the Roman Emperor Probus is reputed to have enjoyed English wines above those from the continent. In fact, he is said to have reinstated vine-growing in Britain after a predecessor had ordered the destruction of British vineyards.

The Venerable Bede's *History of the English People* of the eighth century (later translated by King Alfred) drew from contemporary native records and chronicles as well as from classical sources, and his observation that 'vines are cultivated in several places' is supported by a number of later references. One of King Alfred's laws directed that 'anyone who damaged a vineyard or field belonging to someone else should pay compensation' and there are other tenth-century records in the form of a royal grant of a vineyard to the Abbey of Glastonbury, and mention of vineyards in Anglo-Saxon charters of this time. There are thirty-eight vineyards mentioned in the Domesday Book, some of them of reasonable size, in a wide range of English counties. William of Malmesbury, writing in about 1123, praised Gloucestershire wines highly, and Alexander Necham has a chapter on the vine in his *De Naturis Rerum*. Grapes were gathered in October, which was known as the 'wyn moneth', while pruning was done in February, as illustrated in an Anglo-Saxon manuscript in the British Museum. In some places it was traditional to begin vine pruning on St Vincent's day (22nd January) but Thomas Tusser in 1573 included vine pruning in the tasks allocated to February. Nowadays earlier pruning is usually recommended, and December is considered the best time.

There are many depictions of the vine in art. They occur in countless paintings and engravings of garden scenes throughout the Middle Ages. A representation of the Apocalypse in a fourteenth century French manuscript illustrates a text from Revelations: 'Thrust in thy sharp sickle and gather the clusters of the vine of the earth, for her grapes are fully ripe'. It shows an angel in the clouds instructing a standing angel about to gather the clusters of grapes from a vine trained over a small arbour. A fifteenth-century series of illustrations to the *Decameron* shows a much more elaborate tunnel arbour, big enough for people to walk through, covered in vines and hung with rich bunches of grapes. An Elizabethan wall hanging, stitched in petit point, shows a garden in which laden vines are growing over walls and pillars.

At the beginning of the seventeenth century many of the great gardens had vineyards or vineyard gardens, such as the one at Wimbledon. Sometimes these gardens contained other fruits and flowers as well; the famous Ely vineyard also grew cherries. In *Measure for Measure* the supposed seduction of Isabella is to take place (Act IV sc i)

> *... in a garden circummur'd with brick,*
> *Whose western side is with a vineyard back'd*
> *And to that vineyard is a planched gate,*

That makes his opening with this bigger key.
This other doth command a little door,
Which from the garden to the vineyard leads.

Among the various gardening expenses for the King's garden at
Oatlands in Surrey, there occurs a payment in 1619 'for dressing
and keeping the vines'. Oatlands Palace was a favourite with Queen
Anne of Denmark and there is a portrait of her by Paul van Somer,
showing her in front of the Tuscan style entrance to the vineyard at
Oatlands with the vines just visible in the middle ground of the
painting.

The gardeners of the early seventeenth century knew of a large
number of grapes, so many that Gerard protested 'the which to dis-
tinguish severally were impossible', and even Parkinson noted 'there
is so great diversities . . . I cannot give you names to all that here
grow with us: for John Tradescant my verie good friend, so often
before remembered, hath assured me that he hath twentie sortys
growing with him, that he never knew how or by what name to call
them.' Tradescant introduced several vines not known before to
England, including some of the muscat type which are still grown
for their fine aromatic flavour (though in Britain they sometimes
need extra heat, especially in cooler places). The statesman and gardener Sir William Temple was responsible for bringing in the
'Griselin Frontignac', a muscat which he thought 'the noblest of all
grapes I ever ate in England' though it needed skill to raise: 'it
requires the hottest wall and the sharpest gravel, and must be
favoured by the summer too, to be very good.' Hogg in his 1862
Fruit Manual describes a 'Grizzly Frontignan; and Frontignan is
still a type recommended by the Royal Horticultural Society as a
dessert grape of good flavour. A contemporary painting of Moor
Park in Surrey (attributed to John Kip) shows William Temple's
house and gardens. The extensive fruit garden in the foreground,
stretching the whole of the south side, has a long wall. This would
have been the 'hottest wall', and quite possibly among the plants we
can see trained up it were his delicious Frontignan grapes. Temple
was immensely generous in his gardening and gave away many of
his vines, believing, like many a gardener before and since, that 'of
all things of this kind the commoner they are made the better'.

Much of the grape crop in earlier times went into neither dessert-
fruit nor wine, but was put to the making of verjuice. This acidic

juice made from the green or unripe grapes (or from crab apples) used to be much employed in cooking. One of the earliest vineyard records, from the famous monastery vineyard at Ely, details an account of twenty-seven gallons of verjuice in 1298 and another twenty-one gallons in 1299. The Ely vineyard in Holborn was producing thirty gallons nearly a hundred years later in 1372 and the London vines of the Earl of Lincoln in 1295–6 yielded fifty gallons. In the late sixteenth century, if not earlier, as sharp or as sour as verjuice was an often-used simile, even at times contracted to an adjective as in Heywood's 'She scarce will let me kiss her, But she makes a vergisse face.' It was also held to have medicinal action; Tusser puts in a reminder for a good supply of verjuice:

> Be suer of vergis (a gallon at least),
> so good for the kitchin, so needful for beast.

Sir Hugh Platt who wrote *Floraes Paradise* later republished as *The Garden of Eden*, was a great advocate of grape growing, as was John Rose, gardener to Charles II, and the author of *The English Vineyard Vindicated*. Platt chastised English growers for their poor wine, remarking that they blamed the soil for bad results which came from their lack of skill. Parkinson, too, considered English wines to be rather poor. It is possible that nowadays our good English wines are approaching the quality of the wines which were made by the medieval monks, and surpass the efforts of the seventeenth century. The *Which Guide to Wine*, current at the time I am writing, advises that the English reds are best to avoid, but recommends the whites. The English white wine made at Diss in Suffolk has found its way into the Wine Society's booklet as an outstanding wine of its type. I don't believe that English wines ever were or will be as basic to the culture as they are on the continent, but certain of them make for interesting and agreeable drinking.

Almonds

Almond trees are sold by nurseries all over Britain but they are usually in the 'Ornamental trees' section of the catalogue and only one mentions that the trees bear fruit, noting that the nuts are for culinary use only. England has always imported almonds and walnuts from abroad but in the past there was also a of proportion home-grown nuts. There was a Saxon name for the almond, 'mag-dula treow', probably from the Latin *amygdula*, used in the old scientific name for the tree, *Amygdula communis*. In the Durham Glossary it appears as 'Amigdalus . . . Easterne nute beam' (eastern nut tree). The Oxford English Dictionary quotes a reference for the growing of almonds from before 1300 and there is a recipe involving 'Almond milk', which was popular in Middle Ages and afterwards, in the Babees Book of 1430. There were almonds in the garden of St Gall, and doubtless in many other monastery gardens in the Middle Ages. It is known that considerable quantities were grown at Glastonbury. The gardening list known as the 'Fromond List' (circa 1500) includes almonds, and in 1548 William Turner writes of '*Amygdala* . . . it groweth . . . in England, only in gardines . . .' Later in the sixteenth century Gerard is more specific: 'The natural place of the Almond is in the hot regions, yet we have them in our London gardens and orchards in great plenty.' In the later edition Johnson notes that 'there is a large sweet almond, vulgarly termed a Jordan almond' and there are references to Jordan almonds, which we buy today, going back at least as early as 1440. The term is thought to originate from the French or Spanish for 'garden', be-coming in Middle English *jardyne almaunde* (nothing to do with the country of Jordan with which it later became associated). The Jordan almond is particularly used to make sugared almonds, which are one of the few really old kinds of sweets regularly on sale today. This and some of the other ancient uses for almonds are catalogued by John Parkinson in a delicious list:

> They are used many wayes, and for many purposes, either eaten alone with Figges, or Raysins of the Sunne, or made into paste with Sugar and Rose-water for Marchpanes, or put among Floure, Egges, and Sugar, to make Mackrons, or crusted over with Sugar to make comfits, or mixed with Rosewater and Sugar, to make Butter, or with Barley water, to make Milke . . .

The modern scientific name for almond is *Prunus dulcis*, though you may see its synonmyn *P. amygdalus* (or even *P. communis* or *Amygdalus communis*) in nursery catalogues and books. This is the sort known as the Sweet Almond, pleasant to the taste and unharm-ful. Its cousin, the Bitter Almond (*P. amygdalus* var. *amara*), con-tains much higher concentrations of the glucoside, amygdalin, which when the almonds are eaten turns to prussic acid which can be fatal in quite small doses, so Bitter Almonds should not be eaten.

Garden catalogues of the seventeenth century offered as many as five varieties of almond including the dwarf and the double flowered, both of which are available today. Even in those days almond trees 'were cultivated more for the beauty of their flowers than for its fruit' as Miller remarked in 1735, and significantly even then most catalogues seem to have listed almonds among 'Flowering Trees and Shrubs' rather than with nuts such as the filbert or walnut in the fruit section. It is, however, quite possible to enjoy the nuts as well as the early pink blossom, though in my experience they do not keep well. I gathered about a pound of almonds from the tree on our village green in early December, and the small fruits were very pleasant tasting at that time, but disappointingly, they had shrivelled to nothing by Christmas.

Almonds are fairly short lived trees so they are not often found in old orchards and gardens. However, as they are widely planted for their blossom, they have never really gone out of fashion. In many a town and village garden, their sugar pink blossom is one of the showiest first flowers of spring.

Walnuts

The walnut is long-lived and highly valued for its nuts and wood, and old trees are often seen in orchards and ancient gardens as well as by roads and greens. Nearly all of the nuts in the shops today are imported, but British trees produce very good nuts. It is not a native tree but was planted at an early date (possibly before the Roman occupation), and became naturalized, so homegrown as well as imported nuts have been enjoyed here for many centuries. The Durham Account Rolls include an entry for walnuts, and Langland in Book II of *Piers Plowman* has a metaphor which must refer to homegrown fruits, since the rind is mentioned:

> *For though it be sour to suffer, there comes a sweetness after.*
> *As with a walnut, that has a bitter bark*
> *But after the bitter bark, if it be shelled*
> *There is a kernel of comfort and kindly food.*

The herbalists regarded the walnut highly and adherents of the

doctrine of signatures believed that because of the brainlike appearance of the nut's contents it was efficacious in curing headaches, but
people also enjoyed it simply for the taste. Walnuts occur in a
cookery book of the early fifteenth century: a recipe from 1430
describes the making of 'white fish and walnut sauce'

> Take curnyles of walnotys and clouys of garllek and piper bred and salt and
> cast in a morter and grynd it smal and tempre it with some of the broth that
> the fyshhe was sode in, and serve forth.

There is also a recipe from about 1660 recorded by George
Hartman *(The Family Physician)* which involves preserving green
walnuts in syrup, an interesting idea. The more common use nowadays for green walnuts is pickling. This is also an old tradition but
few of the commercial brands are as delicious as Susannah Avery's
recipe from 1688, which included ginger, bayleaves, mustard seed,
black peppers, horse radish, lemons, cloves and mace.

Walnuts are just as much to be enjoyed in their fresh, natural
state. Tennyson evokes a gentle picture in the *Miller's Daughter*, 'In
after dinner talk/Across the walnuts and the wine', and the artist
William Pyne entitled a series of anecdotes about art *Wine and
Walnuts or After-dinner Chit-chat* (1823). Dorothy Hartley recommends that walnuts should be stored in salt or sand to keep them
fresh.

The seventeenth-century nurserymen, Telfords, listed English
walnuts among 'Forest Trees', although the Virginian Walnut,
known now as the Black Walnut, was included among the 'Ever-
green and Flowering Shrubs. It is quite difficult to get hold of a
named variety of walnut tree nowadays, but Scotts of Merriott not
only stock them, but place them in the Fruit section of their catalogue. They praise the silver-grey bark and the aromatic leaves but
warn that though they have heard of crops occurring after ten years,
it usually takes much longer for walnuts to fruit.

It is traditional that walnuts take a long time to grow and bear
fruit. Thomas Fuller in his *Gnomologia* (1732) quotes a proverb:
'He who plants a walnut tree expects not to eat of the fruit'. (I have,
however, heard of someone who planted a walnut in Suffolk and had
fruit within only a few years.)

Lawrence Hills listed a number of varieties that were sold twenty
years ago, including Excelsior of Taynton, Franquette, Mayette,

Northdown Clawnut, Patching Secrett, and Stutton Seedling. Only a few of these can now be found.

Chestnuts

'Chestnuts of all wilde nuts are the best and meetest to be eaten' wrote William Langham in the *Garden of Health* (1579). Originally from the eastern Mediterranean countries, the sweet chestnut has been grown in Britain at least since the Roman occupation and there are now many wild and semi-wild trees in forests as well as in culti-vated plantations. There are large coppice woods of sweet chestnut, especially in Kent, but they are grown to provide poles for hop-growing and for fencing rather than for their fruit.

Most of the Christmas chestnuts that we find on sale are im-ported, often from Italy, although they are known as Spanish Chest-nuts. In the past, chestnuts were grown in Britain for their nuts (strictly speaking seeds, rather than nuts). There are references in twelfth- and thirteenth-century accounts of nuts having been sent in considerable quantities to the royal households. Gardeners in the south of Britain can still raise good crops of chestnuts although since the sweet chestnut is a very large tree and spreads heavy shade, it can only be taken on where there is plenty of space. The chestnuts, like those we gather in woods, tend to be a little smaller and less full than their foreign counterparts, but they can be very sweet and tasty and can be eaten fresh before they have time to get rubbery.

Hazel

The woodland hazel is a native tree, valued for its nuts, pliant branches and wood before history began to be written. There is also another kind of hazel, an imported species known as the filbert. This too appears to have been grown in Britain from an early date, for there are written references to it as far back as the thirteenth cen-tury. Filberts were rated more highly than the native cobnuts (thought to have been so called because they are short and round, or 'cobby'). John Parkinson described the distinctive characteristics of the two kinds of hazel beginning with the filberts, whose nuts

are wholly enclosed in long, thicke, rough huskes, bearded as it were at the
upper ends, or cut into divers jagges, much more than the wood nut: the nut
hath a thinne and somewhat hard shell, but not so thicke and hard as the
wood nut, in some longer than the other, and in the long kinde, one hath, the
skinne white that covereth the kernels, and another red.

Filberts, he emphasized were eaten as 'the best kinde of Hasell nuts,
at bankets among other dainty fruits'.

John Evelyn also thought filberts 'a kinder and better sort of
Hazel-nut', fit to be brought 'to the best Tables for Desert', and he
recommends a pudding made out of either cobnuts or filberts (pre-
ferably the latter) which he esteems as highly as that made from
more expensive almonds.

There are a number of varieties of both the cob and the filbert,
some of which are still obtainable. The Red Filbert and the White
Filbert were known as far back as the late sixteenth century but the
most famous filbert, originally called Lambert's Filbert because it
was raised by Mr Lambert of Goudhurst in Kent, was introduced
about 1830. This is the nut which is now known as the Kentish
Cob, although it is the non-native species *Corylus maxima*. The indigenous cobs are not so widely cultivated but one good variety with
a large oblong nut and sweet flavour is the Cosford, introduced from
Ipswich in 1816.

CHAPTER FOUR

Garden Berries and Wild Harvests

Wife unto thy garden, and set me a plot,
With strawberry rootes of the best to be got:
Such growing abroad, among thornes in a wood
Wel chosen and picked, proove excellent good.

The barberry, respis and gooseberry too,
Look now to be planted, as other things do:
The gooseberry, respis, and roses all three,
With strawberries under them trimly agree.

ALL OF THE PLANTS mentioned here by Thomas Tusser, in his Good Husbandry lessons for September, may still be found growing wild in woods and hedgerows, much as they did in the sixteenth century when Tusser wrote these verses. They may all be considered native plants. (There is some argument about the status of the barberry, but there is a good case for accepting it as native to certain parts of Britain.) There are also other native wild plants which have been taken into gardens and tentatively brought under cultivation, such as bilberries and cranberries. Others again, such as sloes, elderberries and rowanberries, remain decidedly a wild harvest. We still forage for such plants much as our ancestors did for thousands of years before us.

Strawberries

Most cultivated fruits are bigger than their wild relatives, some through cross-breeding with foreign species, others through a continuous history of gardeners' selection through the centuries.

Tusser, as we see, was quite clear on the origins of his garden strawberries. He directed Mrs T. to the woods to dig up wild ones. By
Parkinson's time there must have been room for doubt about the
provenance of these larger garden plants for he feels bound to say:
'I must enforme you that the wilde Strawberry that groweth in the
Woods is our Garden strawberry, but bettered by the soyle and
transplanting.'

There are references to strawberries all the way back to the
Anglo-Saxon herbal manuscripts and the glossary of Aelfric. They
were clearly greatly enjoyed hundreds of years before they were sold
on the streets and in markets during the seventeenth century, and
recommended by Parkinson as a 'pleasant dish' in the summer season 'wherunto claret wine, creame or milke is added with sugar'. It
is perhaps no accident that in Richard Dering's arrangement of
London Street Cryes (1630) 'I have fresh cheese and cream, I have
fresh' is followed directly by 'I have ripe strawberries ripe'. Izaak
Walton, who appreciated the strawberry, recorded for posterity
Doctor William Butler's memorable words upon the subject:
'doubtless God could have made a better berry, but doubtless God
never did'.

Nowadays the little wild strawberry is rarely seen in gardens
except in the form of the alpine strawberry, a subspecies from the
European Alps. It is, of course, now illegal to transplant strawberries from the wild as Tusser directed, but why should one bother,
when they are abundant in woods and grassland throughout many
parts of the British Isles? A Swedish way of collecting wild strawberries is to thread them on to a long stalk of summer grass. Wild
strawberries are more delicious than the modern garden kinds; they
have a piquancy of taste which offsets the sweetness. The whole process of collecting wild strawberries – the waiting for ripeness, the
excursion, the searching-out and gathering of the little red berries;
and all the sights, sounds and odours of a summer day – becomes
involved with the enjoyment of eating them. I find that these associations linger even with alpine and wild strawberries gathered from
the garden, and I always enjoy these more than the larger and more
succulent garden cultivars.

The strawberries we at present grow in our gardens, so much
larger and sweeter than their wild relatives, are the result of considerable interbreeding between strawberry species, principally the
North American *Fragaria virginiana* and the South American

Fragaria chiloensis. It is interesting that the former had been introduced by the early seventeenth century and that John Parkinson had some in his garden, of which he reported downheartedly: 'with want of skill, or industry to order it aright scarce can one Strawberry be seene ripe among a number of plants.' However, by the late eighteenth century the hybrid stock upon which most of our garden strawberries are founded was established.

The kinds of strawberry which we can obtain nowadays are mostly recent, dominated by the range of Cambridge varieties developed over the last fifty years. Bunyard describes eighty-six different varieties of the older sorts which were sold in 1925 but of these only one, the Royal Sovereign introduced by the Laxton nurseries in 1892, is now available. It is still considered one of the finest-flavoured strawberries but the crop is smaller than that of the less tasty varieties. Bright red, with a pale flesh, the Royal Sovereign brought about a kind of revolution in colour in strawberries; the fashion throughout the nineteenth century had been for a dark berry. Most ordinary varieties of strawberry are susceptible to virus disease and it is always wisest to buy certified stocks, rather than to propagate your own. Remontant strawberries (also called Perpetual or Ever-bearing) are not available as certified stock, but a gardener selecting strong, healthy runners from mature plants, can expect a reasonably good crop in the future. Some of the alpine strawberries breed true to seed, but they can also be increased by splitting. They were introduced to cultivation in 1760, and since 1825, when varieties without runners were discovered, this is the form in which you usually find them nowadays. The best-flavoured is generally thought to be Baron Solemacher which fruits (in common with most alpines) over a long period. I have pulled the first berries in May and still been gathering from this variety in October.

Raspberries

The common raspberry, the European red raspberry, is one of the few commonly cultivated fruits which tastes recognizably the same inside a garden and when it is found in the wild. Wild raspberries are, as is usually the case, smaller, and their fruits are sparser, but the wild species and all of the garden varieties share the same exciting sharpness of taste. In *Hesperides*, Herrick writes of 'The wine of

Cherries and the cooling breach of Respasses'. Raspberries, like strawberries, were grown in the past both for medicinal purposes and as a dessert fruit, and in the latter role they appear to have been enjoyed at tea-time, as John Parkinson observed: 'The berries are eaten in Summer time, as an afternoon's dish, to please the taste of the sicke as well as the sound.' Raspberry juice, conserve and syrup were also popular during his time.

Turner in 1548 notes an ancient English name for raspberries which is still used in the north, 'raspeses or hyndberies'. He also remarked that 'they growe . . . in certayne gardines of Englande.' They appear to have been widely cultivated. Gerard and Parkinson as well as Turner and Tusser mention raspberries in gardens, and in his best known poem, *Fair Virtue or The Mistress of Philarette* (1622), George Wither describes 'shrubbie fields' or 'Raspice Orchards'.

There are virtually no old varieties of raspberry now available, though some were sold up to the middle of this century. From Aberdeen to Exeter, the raspberry lists of nursery catalogues are dominated by the hardy range of Mallings and the autumn-fruiting variety called September. There is only one old kind to be found, a healthy New Zealand clone of the variety Lloyd George.

In his 1862 edition of *The Fruit Manual* Hogg listed a large range of summer and autumn raspberries of black, red and yellow kinds. I can remember eating marvellous yellow raspberries in an old kitchen garden in Amersham, but since the Yellow Antwerp (known to Hogg) disappeared from the catalogues, only the inferior Golden Everest remains, and even this is becoming difficult to find. Black raspberries seem to have disappeared completely.

Blackberries

'Who has not been in his day a Blackberry gatherer?' pondered J. E. Smith, author of the celebrated *Sowerby's English Botany*. It was only at the end of the nineteenth century that the verb 'to blackberry' established itself in the English language, but it describes a human activity with a history of thousands of years. It was no surprise to paleobotanists to discover blackberry pips amongst other wild foods in the stomach contents of a person from the Neolithic period. When we gather blackberries from the scratchy wild brambles, we are in a real sense on an equal footing with the early foragers, as in few other modern day activities. The popularity of this wild harvest shows no sign of waning, and blackberrying is a seasonal ritual for people both of town and country. As for serving them at table, there can be few fruit dishes as simple and as tasty as wild blackberries stewed lightly with cooking or crab apples and laced with honey, or a well-packed traditional blackberry pie.

Garden blackberries are sugary-sweet, oversized and watery by comparison with the tart wild kinds. Nurseries stock several varieties such as Himalyan Giant, Bedford Giant and John Innes but there is actually more choice in the wild, with an estimated two thousand microspecies of the common wild blackberry and the dewberry (also called 'the token blackberry' because of its small size).

Species of *Rubus* cross-breed readily with each other and a number of hybrid berries have arisen out of both intentional and accidental crossings. The most famous of these, the loganberry, was raised by a Judge Logan of California in 1881, from a cross between the raspberry (subspecies *strigosus*) and *Rubus vitifolius*, a Californian blackberry.

Bilberries

Greater size and sweetness usually seem to be the aims of garden cultivators and nurserymen, but there are other fruits besides blackberries which people have traditionally gathered wild. The native wild bilberry has at times been grown in gardens, but for most people it is impossible to think of it other than as a plant of the moorlands. In many places bilberries are still known by the old country names of whortleberry and hurtleberry. They were regarded as a delicacy even in the sixteenth century when, as Gerard noted: 'The people of Cheshire do eat blacke wortles in creame and milke, as in these South parts we eate Strawberries. . . .' Dorothy Hartley, who considered bilberry tarts to be simply 'the best on earth', recollected, that on certain moors there were rights to gather bilberries. This is a slow, blue-staining fidgety job if you are gathering seriously and in large quantities. Large parties of gypsies or villagers go up on the moors to pick all day, and are met in the evening by a farm lorry which takes back their full baskets.

Bilberries are also known as blueberries in some parts of the north of England, and they are sometimes confused with the plant of the same name on sale in some nurseries. The nursery blueberries are in fact the American species *(Vaccinium corymbosum* and *V. ashei)* known as High Bush blueberries. The fruits are twice as large as our bilberries, but for my taste inferior in flavour, oversweet and cloying, a disappointment when set against the reputation of American blueberry pie. How far our bilberries remain a truly wild harvest may be seen from the fact that I can find no nursery which currently sells our native bilberry, though some used to do so up until quite recently. A number of varieties of the American species may be obtained from a few stockists.

Cranberries

The name 'cranberry' also signifies separate, though related, species in Britain and America. However, to most people the cranberry is the large American kind, *Vaccinium macrocarpum,* the one generally eaten with turkey at Christmas, and sold in nurseries. Our own native cranberry, *Vaccinium oxycoccus,* a slender graceful bogland plant which has tiny, sharp-tasting berries, grows wild, largely unseen and unrecognized, although this was not always the case. The *Child's Guide to Knowledge,* a long catechism of improving questions and answers written by 'A Lady' of considerable Victorian gravity, put it thus in my 1871 edition:

Q What are Cranberries?
A A small red fruit about the size of a pea, which grows
   in the fens in the north of England, Lincolnshire, and
   Cambridgeshire.
Q Is not the collecting of cranberries a disagreeable employment?
A Yes; for each berry grows on a separate stalk, and the
   gathering is damp, dirty work.
Q What town is famous for them?
A Longtown, in Cumberland: their rich flavour is generally esteemed.
Q Are not many brought to this country from North America and Russia?
A Yes; they are a larger fruit, but not so pleasant.

English cranberry sauce needs considerable sweetening, even for those who like a sharp taste. It is a delicacy restricted mainly to those who live near the places where cranberries grow wild, in the north of England and Wales.

Another red berry with a sharp taste, closely related to the cranberry (sometimes hybridising with it) is the cowberry, otherwise known as the mountain cranberry. A plant which is in a different genus, but which resembles Heath family plants, is the crowberry. This pretty little low-growing undershrub has very small pink flowers which are followed by berries which eventually turn black. These are edible, but not very tasty. Just recently there has been an unexpected increase in this plant on Ilkley Moor, but even with an abundance of berries, it seems that local people have not yet discovered appetising ways of serving them.

Gooseberries

Come all ye jovial gardeners, and listen unto me,
Whilst I relate the different sorts of winning gooseberries
This famous institution was founded long ago,
That men might meet, and drink, and have a gooseberry show.

*   *   *

There's Dan's Mistake and Catherina, Magenta and Careless too,
Clayton, Drill, and Telegraph, Antagonist and Peru;
Mount Pleasant, Plunder, King of Trumps, Australia and Railway,
Ploughboy, High Sheriff, and Gretna Green; but the Bobby wins the day.

There's Speedwell, Leader, Matchless, Freedom and Slaughterman.
Queen of Trumps and Trumpeter, Surprise and Nottingham,
Duke of Sutherland, Lord Ratcliffe, Garibaldi and Eskender Bey,
Jenny Lind and Dr Hogg; but the Bobby wins the day.

The Gooseberry Growers' Song

There are a great many other verses of this song (featured in the *Gooseberry Growers' Register* of 1885) which includes the names of some of the most famous gooseberry varieties grown in the eighteenth and nineteenth centuries. In his *Guide to the Orchard and Kitchen Garden* (1831), Lindley pays tribute to 'the gentlemen of Lancashire' who 'raised Gooseberries remarkable for size and flavour', and he lists no less than 722 varieties categorized by their colours as Reds, Yellows, Greens and Whites.

Gooseberry clubs began to be founded about 1740 for the raising and exhibition of specimen gooseberries. Although the show specimens were huge fruits, the size of ping-pong balls, many of the show varieties were of excellent taste. The first annual register was made in 1786 and the competition was fierce. The story of the winning gooseberries, told in the *Growers' Song*, celebrates the outstanding varieties: Lion in the early part of the nineteenth century, which gave way to London and then to Bobby. The London gooseberry was unique in being champion no less than thirty-one times between 1839 and 1897. Many of the varieties in the register were prefixed by the grower's own name, such as Reeve's Dreadnought, Farmer's Roaring Lion, Lovart's Elisha (red) and Elijah (green), Shelmardine's Cheshire Stag and Taylor's No Bribery. Though most of the dessert varieties have disappeared, some of the famous gooseberry names still with us were bred by the gooseberry clubs. Leveller and Careless gooseberries were both 'let out' in 1851.

Gooseberries are native plants and can still be found growing wild over most of Britain in woods and hedgerows, by streams and scrubland. A friend of mine showed me a thriving gooseberry bush growing in the crotch of a pollard willow, and in a little wood close to where I live, there is a gooseberry bush growing beneath an ancient beech tree, which bears quantities of small sharp-tasting fruit in the mid summer.

Gooseberries were grown in gardens in the early Middle Ages. A bill from the reign of Edward I shows that some gooseberries were imported between 1276 and 1292 from France for cultivation in the garden at Westminster. It seems likely that we imported also the name 'gooseberry' from the French *groseille*. In modern French *groseiller* is a currant bush, yielding *groseilles à grappes*, which are red or white currants. The gooseberry is *groseille à maquereau*, a suitable name, for then as now gooseberry sauce is rated as the best accompaniment for mackerel. A number of recipes survive from the early eighteenth century, such as the delicious gooseberry tansy made with eggs, breadcrumbs and gooseberries, and gooseberry fool, which is still considered a most excellent dessert. In her pioneering cookery book Eliza Acton has a recipe for 'grosellée', a preserve made from ripe gooseberries and raspberry juice.

Gooseberry idioms still in use seem more likely to hark back to French than to English tradition, although their origins are obscure. To 'be a gooseberry', in the sense of a chaperone or unwelcome third

Mulberry

Black Currant

Red Currant

White Currant

Coe's Golden Drop

Damson

Greengage

Cherry Plum

party, is a relatively modern use of an expression which previously meant to act as a go-between. Perhaps the fact that the French *maquereau* (or *-elle*) was slang for a pimp suggested this use. As for babies being 'found under a gooseberry bush', this is more obscure, though perhaps it involved wordplay on the notion of pregnancy (in French a pregnant woman is *une femme grosse* and the gooseberry *groseille*).

Gerard gives an alternative name for the gooseberry: feaberry. This appears in other documents as fayberny, fabes, fapes, feaps and thapes and thebes, from the sixteenth century to the mid-twentieth, when Evelyn Waugh wrote of 'feaberry cake'. This group of names may derive from the old English word *theve*, meaning a prickly shrub. In Norfolk, the word feaberry is applied only to unripe berries, perhaps because wild gooseberries are similar in taste to sharp, unripe cultivated ones.

Turner mentions garden gooseberries in his *Names of Herbes* (1548), and there is a royal record from the time of Henry VIII (1516) when the 'pale' gooseberry was introduced from France. Parkinson records 'three red gooseberries, a blew and an greene', but it is impossible to match his short descriptions with any of the varieties we know nowadays. I am fond of greeny flowers, and the small blooms of the gooseberry are among my favourites. Horticultural writers usually ignore fruit flowers unless they are unusually showy, but Parkinson describes gooseberry blossom very clearly:

> the flowers come forth single, at everie joint of the leaf one or two, of a purplish green colour, hollow and turning up the brims a little: the berries follow, bearing the flowers on the heads of them, which are of a pale green at the first and of a greenish yellow colour when ripe, striped in divers places, and cleare, almost transparent . . .

By the time of the famous fifth edition of Evelyn's combined *Sylva* and *Pomona*, several other varieties were known: Amber Great, Early Red, English Yellow and Great Yellow. Another variety, mentioned in the Appendix to Evelyn's *Pomona*, is the 'Crystal': a variety which seems to have been so well liked that the Warwickshire squire and poet, William Somerville included it in his '*Hobbinal, or The Rural Games, a Burlesque Poem*':

> ... *Chrystal gooseberries*
> *Are piled on heaps, in vain the parent tree*
> *Defends her luscious fruit with pointed spears.*

A variety named White Crystal is also to be found in George Lindley's gooseberry list of 1831, and the name Crystal also occurs in Hogg's *Fruit Manual* (1862), describing a white variety which might be the same as the old kind.

There are two nurseries in Britain which specialize in the old varieties of gooseberry, and their catalogues include about fifty varieties which go back a hundred years or so. Among these are Crown Bob, Hearts of Oak, Roaring Lion, Green Walnut and many others mentioned by Hogg. One gooseberry mentioned by William Forsyth in 1802 and still highly esteemed for its flavour, is the Golden Drop, a delicious yellow variety.

Gooseberries have a marked affinity with the flowers of the elder. A head of elderflowers tied in muslin and cooked with the goose-berries for a fool changes the taste in an indefinable but delicious way, and there are recipes for gooseberry jam made with elder flowers, which produce a preserve of extraordinary distinction.

Currants

The French name for red and white currants, *groseille à grappes*, seems to have influenced a number of country names in Britain, such as gazels in Kent, and rizzels and russles in parts of Scotland. The word 'currant' has referred both to fresh currants and to the dried grapes used in cake-making for several centuries, as Gerard made clear when he added to his description of 'Ribes or Red Currans' –

> yet they must not be confounded with those Currans, which are brought from Xant [the Greek island] and the continent adjoining thereto, and which are vulgarly sold by our grocers; for they are the fruit of a small Vine, and differ much from these.

In the sixteenth century, the word 'raisin' was similarly ambiguous. Turner in his *Names of Herbes* (1548) described the red currant bush as 'Rhibes, called in some places of Englande a Rasin tree'; and when Thomas Tusser included 'reisons' among the plants to be set or removed in January in his *Five Hundred Points of Good Husbandry* (1573), he almost certainly meant red or white currants.

These currants, now becoming scarce, expensive and briefly available in shops, are not difficult to grow. Garden red currants are derived from two wild species: the wild red currant *(Ribes sylvestre)* and the closely related downy currant *(R. spicatum)*. The downy currant is certainly native to Britain, the red is very likely so. Another wild species, the mountain currant *(R. alpinum)*, was cultivated in the past (which accounts for feral populations in some unlikely places), but it had no part in the genetics of modern garden currants.

The garden red currant, with its scintillating sweet-sour taste, is not only one of the most delicious of fruits, but also the most beautiful. Only the glistening red fruits of the wild guelder rose can rival red currants, and the red currant has a more refined clarity, a purer translucence. 'Red as a Cherry when . . . ripe', Parkinson observed, 'of a pleasant and tart taste'. Perhaps it was for aesthetic reasons as well as for the combination of tastes that cherries and currants were served together. Among the several poems which Richard Lovelace dedicated 'To Ellinda' was one celebrating 'Being Treated' which begins

> *For Cherries plenty, and for Coran's*
> *Enough for fifty . . .*

Eliza Acton recommends a 'compote of red currants' using a very little water and adding some sugar; she also mixes red currants and raspberries together, a combination which creates a splendid piquancy in the best summer puddings and fruit salads.

White currants are a variety of the red currant (occasionally white currants occur in the wild species). They are usually rather less sharp in taste, and, Parkinson thought 'more accepted and desired, as also because they are more daintie, and less common'. Eliza Acton has a recipe for a 'Very Fine White Currant Jelly'. Many of us would be pleased to have access to the modest six pounds of fruit which this requires, for they are virtually unobtainable in shops. Private fruit gardeners are almost the only people still to know how this pearly little fruit tastes.

A number of nurseries sell varieties of white currants and of some of the older red currants. White Dutch is mentioned both by Hogg (1862) and Lindley (1831), though it is known that a number of varieties bore this name. White Versailles, raised in 1843, is thought to be the sweetest white and a very good garden variety; it was recommended as generously by Harry Baker of the Royal Horti-cultural Society in 1980 as it was by George Bunyard at the turn of the century.

The black currant *(Ribes nigrum)* is another bush native to Britain and is found in woods, hedges and fens. The diminutive flowers, unobtrusive like the other flowers of the *Ribes* family, are nonetheless attractive in their own way: 'like unto little bottles . . . of a greenish purple colour, which turn into blacke berries' wrote the observant Parkinson who so much appreciated flowers of all kinds. Most writers past and present remark on the strong scent of blackcurrant leaves. Some of them, John Evelyn included, thought of the fruit purely in medicinal terms. Parkinson was a little more open-minded though scarcely effusive: 'both branches leaves and fruit have a kind of stinking sent with them, yet are not unwholesome, but are eaten of many, without offending either taste or smell'. The soothing pro-perties of blackcurrants for coughs and sore throats and their high vitamin C content are well-known to us today, though the old country name of quinsy berry has fallen out of use.

Of the black currants, Black Naples is a name which occurs during the nineteenth century and which Bunyard believes is synonymous with Baldwin, still available nowadays. Other later nineteenth-century varieties include Boskoop Giant and Blacksmith. A variety with a useful resistance to the common 'big bud' disease (black cur-rant gall mite) is Seabrook's Black, an old variety, reintroduced by Seabrook in 1913.

Barberry

The barberry is a fruit which has vanished from our tables and (except in the form of an exotic ornamental) from our gardens. The common barberry *(Berberis vulgaris)* grows into a stout bush whose pendant flowers turn into long, oval berries, brilliant red when ripe, and, as Parkinson describes them, 'of a sharpe taste, fit to set their teeth on edge that eat them'. They do, however, make an excellent sauce for fish or meat, and were grown for this purpose from the sixteenth century onwards. In his *New Art of Gardening* (1732) Leonard Meager defends the barberry's right to a 'Place in an Orchard by Reason of the Usefulness of its Fruit on Sundry Occasions'. They can be candied for decorations on sweet dishes, pickled in brine, or made into a beautiful amber-red jelly to accompany mutton. Mrs Beeton adds that 'the berries arranged on bunches of nice curled parsley make an exceedingly pretty garnish for white meats'.

Barberries will grow well in any soil, and, according to Gerard in 1597, were 'planted in most places in England'. He observed that they also thrived in the wild and at field edges, whereas William Turner in 1548 knew them 'onely in gardines'. Barberries were quite often to be seen in hedgerows until fairly recently, when it was discovered that the bushes are subject to a rust – the ascidial stage of Black Rust (*Puccinia graminis*) which attacks cereal crops, principally wheat – and a strong campaign for the eradication of wild barberry bushes was carried out in wheat-growing districts. I know of one hedge, pointed out to me by a friend, where there are several good barberry bushes; these happen to grow between two wheat-fields with both species apparently undiseased. Yet, though it may be wiser not to grow barberry in the neighbourhood of cereal crops, it would be a shame if the cultivation of this fruit died out altogether. I do not know of any nurseries which stock the common barberry but it will grow from seed which can be gathered from wild bushes.

The Birds in the Bush

Soft fruits are as attractive to birds as they are to human beings. Some gardeners are obsessive on the subject and go to enormous lengths to keep birds away with poles and cages and nets, to the extent of making their fruit gardens resemble army obstacle courses. These tense and nervy places are a far cry from the sanctuaries of refuge and meditation that gardens represented in the past. Some old English gardening books actually counted birds among the pleasures of the orchard. Ralph Austen found it

> . . . a pleasure to the eare to heare the sweet notes and tunes of singing birds, whose company a man shall be sure to have in an orchard, which is more pleasant there than elsewhere, because of other concurrent pleasures there; a concert of musick is more pleasant than upon a single instrument.

William Lawson, too, had a word of appreciation for particular birds among his list of the delightful benefits of an orchard:

One chief grace that adorns an Orchard, I cannot let slip: a brood of Nightingales, who with several notes and tunes, with a strong delightsome voice out of a weak body, will bear you company night and day . . . She will help you to cleanse your trees of Caterpillars, and all noysome worms and flies. The gentle Robin-red-brest will help her, and in winter in the coldest storms will keep apart. Neither will the silly Wren be behind in Summer, with her distinct whistle (like a sweet Recorder) to chear you spirits.

Lawson could even see a good side to the thrush family (the blackbird, song thrush and mistle thrush), though his appreciation of their springtime song did not blur his perception of the late-season damage they might wreak.

The Black-bird and Throstle (for I take it the Thrush sings not but devours) sing loudly in a May morning, and delights the ear much, and you need not want their company, if you have ripe Cherries or Berries, and would as gladly as the rest do your pleasure: but I had rather want their company than my fruit.

In an earlier chapter in which Lawson deals with the army of mischiefs (including human ones) which can afflict an orchard, birds once again figure and the problems and defence measures read more like those of modern times.

Your Cherries, and other Berries, when they be ripe, will draw all the Blackbirds, Thrushes, and Mag-pies to your Orchard. The Bul-finch is a devourer of your fruit in the bud, I have had whole Trees shall'd out with them in Winter-time.

The best remedy here is a Stone bow, a Piece, especially if you have a musket, or sparrow hawk in winter, to make the Black-bird stoop into a bush or hedge.

Forsyth (1831) has two chapters on the problems which can afflict fruit trees and bushes, the first on 'Mildew, Honey Dew and Blights', and the second on 'Insects, Aphis, Caterpillars, Moths, Ants, Earwigs, Slugs, Snails, Wasps and Flies, Rats and Mice.' Even hawk moths get a longer mention than birds in this volume. Forsyth protects his fruit from birds by a method which doubles in helping protect it from frost:

When fruit begins to ripen, Birds will attack it. The best preventative in this case is, to cover the trees with nets, or buntine, a sort of cloth of which ships colours are made. These will admit a free circulation of air to the fruit, and will soon dry after rain: they will also be a good covering for the trees in Spring, in cold, wet, or snowy weather.

But Forsyth recognizes that birds can be a pleasure:

Those who are fond of the natural harmony of singing-birds will find Barberries well adapted for attracting them to the spots where they are planted, most birds being very fond of them.

Almost all later gardening books, however, seem to treat birds exclusively as enemies, although some organic gardeners have good words for them at least at the beginning of the year, when birds such as tits pick off insects which attack young buds and leaves. At the time when fruit is ripe and vulnerable there is little difference in the advice given by gardeners of any period. This is a modern organic gardener, Lawrence Hills, describing the bird pillagers who

turn on our fruit . . . there is only one way to beat really determined birds, and that is a fruit cage. The old type had wire netting sides, and this has to be smaller than two-inch mesh, for the modern bird simply flies straight at large mesh netting, declutches, folds wings, coasts through, engages third and accelerates away on the other side. Birds have learned to deal with wire netting of wider than body size as easily as with milk bottles. Wire netting rusts with time and is relatively costly, but today it is being rapidly replaced with nylon netting.

Caging birds instead of fruit, and having aviaries in gardens, is a custom which has gone in and out of fashion at least since the sixteenth century. Some of these aviaries were huge, as at Kenilworth. Francis Bacon, the arbiter of good taste in gardens, had no liking for them nor did many poets. The bird whose song 'made hevy hertes light' and ravished the gardener in Lydgate's poem *The Churl and his Bird* refused to sing when caught and put in a cage. The beautiful garden in Chaucer's *The Romaunt of the Rose* was full both of birds and of fruits, and one of the most delightful passages in the contemporaneous *Flower and the Leaf* is the description of the goldfinch in the blossoming medlar tree.

Personally, I prefer a garden to be a scene of pleasant delight rather than a zoo of fruit cages and nets. A little discreet netting at critical times is useful, but on the whole, I don't grudge the birds a share of the harvest. It seems mean-minded to welcome thrushes and blackbirds in the winter and then to begrudge them a tithe in the fruitful months.

CHAPTER FIVE

The Kindes or Sorts of Apples

The Summer pippin is a very good apple first ripe, and therefore to be first spent, because it will not abide so long as the other.

The Golding pippin is the greatest and best of all sorts of pippins.

The spotted pippin is the most durable pippin of all the other sorts.

The great pearemaine differeth little either in taste or durabilitie from the pippin, and therefore next unto it is accounted the best of all apples.

The summer pearemaine is of equall goddness with the former, or rather a little more pleasing, especially for the time of its eating, which will not bee so long lasting, but is spent and gone when the other beginneth to be good to eate.

The Broading is a very good apple.

The Flower of Kent is a faire yellowish greene apple both good and great.

The Gilloflower apple is a fine apple, and finely spotted.

The Gruntlin is somewhat a long apple, smaller at the crowne than at the stalke, and a reasonable good apple.

The gray Costard is a good great apple, somewhat whitish on the outside, and abideth the winter.

The Belle boon of two sorts winter and summer, both of them good apples, and fair fruit to look on, being yellow and of a meane bignesse.

The Dousan or apple John is a delicate fine fruit, well relished when it beginneth to be fit to be eaten, and endureth good longer then any other apple.

The Spicing is a well tasted fruite.

The Queen apple is of two sorts, both of them great faire apples, and well relished, but the greater is the best.

The Pot apple is a plaine Country apple.

The Cowsnout is no very good fruit.

The Cats head apple tooke the name of the likenesse, and is a reasonable good apple and great.

The Kentish Codlin is a faire great greenish apple, very good to eate when it is ripe; but the best to coddle of all other apples.

The Geneting apple is a very pleasant and good apple.
The old wife is a very good, and well relished apple.
The towne Crab is an hard apple, not so good to be eaten rawe as roasted,
    but excellent to make Cider.
The Sugar apple is so called of the sweetnesse.
Sops in wine is so named both of the pleasantness of the fruit, and beautie of
    the apple.
Twenty sorts of Sweetings and none good.

This is a selection from John Parkinson's chapter on apples in the *Paradisus*. Its purpose was simply to list some of the apples available at the time, but I have always felt it to be a kind of poem. There is a reassuring substantiality in the balanced cadences of the seventeenth-century sentences, and a sense of permanence in the knowledge that many apples known by these old names can still be found. You will have to grow them yourself, but since there is a wider range of old apples to be found in nurseries than there is of any other fruit, this is one case in which gardeners have an excellent choice.

If you want basic information about almost any apple you know by name, there is a remarkable modern inventory of varieties written by Muriel Smith, *The National Apple Register of the United Kingdom*, published by the Ministry of Agriculture, Fisheries and Food. If it is the Bible of apple kinds, it must be called the 'New English Bible'. But if its prose does not compare with Parkinson's, the information compressed into its terse entries is considerable: about six thousand separate cultivars are identified and described, with notes on their status and provenance. Yet even with this huge coverage the *Apple Register* is not quite exhaustive, and not infrequently one finds a variety which has escaped its formidable trawl.

Although the apple took first place in John Gardener's verse treatise on the grafting of fruit trees, and other early English gardening books dealt with it fully, it seems that it was not until the early eighteenth century that the feeling was openly articulated that the apple is a fruit of special significance to the English. Richard Bradley wrote in his *New Improvements of Planting and Gardening* (1718) 'There is no kind of Fruit better known in England than the Apple, or more generally cultivated. It is of that Use that I hold it almost impossible for the English to live without it, whether it be employed for that excellent Drink we call cyder, or for the many Dainties which are made of it in the Kitchen.' Its special 'Englishness' is not simply the result of apples growing particularly well in the British climate; for centuries the British have been expert in apples, appreciating their subtle differences and discriminating in favour of quality and variety. Not only was a wide spectrum of dessert apples perfected by a very early date, but the sharp distinctions between one cooking apple and another, all but ignored in other countries, were explored and exploited. It is still possible to find nurseries offering eighty or more kinds of dessert apple and perhaps thirty kinds for cooking.

The Origins of Fame

In his long poem of the English countryside, *Poly-Olbion* (1613), Michael Drayton mentions a number of famous apple varieties by name, including the Apple-Orenge, Russetting, Peare-maine Costard and Pomwater. Before he leaves the subject, he pays tribute to the regional varieties, 'sundry other fruits of good yet severall taste / That have their sundry names in sundry counties plac't'. There is still considerable pride taken in local varieties of apple. The Bramley, our best-known, best-loved cooking apple, originated in the little cathedral town of Southwell in the early nineteenth century. There is a pub there called the Bramley Apple which serves traditional apple pie, and the original Southwell Bramley tree is still alive: indeed a graft was taken from it for the National Fruit Trials.

In my own garden there is an old Lane's Prince Albert, a variety sold all over the country because it is such a reliable cropper and good cooker, and hardy in the north. It has a special significance in our area, however, because it originated in a Berkhamsted garden in the mid-nineteenth century. It was introduced by the local firm of Lane and named after the Prince Consort.

Some apples reach their peak only in their own region, a fact emphasized by John Parkinson four hundred and fifty years ago: 'some [varieties] are more familiar to one Countrey then to another, being of a better or worse taste in one place then in another.' Such a one is the D'Arcy Spice, a richly aromatic russet apple, also known as the Essex Spice, which dates at least as far back as the eighteenth century and is still to be found in many Essex gardens. It was originally discovered in the gardens of the Hall at Tolleshunt d'Arcy. I should love to grow a D'Arcy Spice but I fear I should not have it at its best in the soil conditions of my part of Hertfordshire.

The most famous apple to be raised in the gardens of an English country house is the Ribston pippin. The seed from which it was grown is said to have come from France and was planted at Ribston Hall, near Knaresborough, at the beginning of the eighteenth century. There are two pen and ink drawings of the Hall by an unidentified artist, probably dating from a little before 1707, which might have allowed us a unique glimpse into this famous garden at the time the young Ribstons were planted. However, its owner, Sir Henry Goodricke, had gone to the extraordinary pains of 'environing his garden with a kind of fortification' and in these drawings of the Hall, the solid high walls stand in the way of our seeing into the garden beyond a tantalizing glimpse of some fan-trained fruit on the far walls. The Ribston pippin was once the best-loved dessert apple in Britain but its popularity was superseded by its offspring, the Cox's orange pippin, raised about 1825 by Richard Cox, a retired brewer of Colnbrook in Buckinghamshire.

The most ancient cultivated apples that we know about, and which are still grown, are said to have been brought over by the Romans: the Pomme d'Api and the Court Pendu Plat. Court Pendu Plat is a small, very late-flowering and late-fruiting tree which gives a generous crop of smallish, red-flushed apples, crisp, sweet and perfumed. It is still quite widely grown on the continent, though it is available from only very few nurseries in Britain. I have not yet found the Pomme d'Api on any nurseryman's list, but this small, tender sweet apple is in the collection at the National Fruit Trials and a graft can be arranged for people who specially want this variety. This is also a late season apple though not so late as the Court Pendu Plat.

Apples for a Garden

There is such a wide choice of apples, and so many ways of growing them, that even in a small garden one can have an exquisite selection, grown in different forms – as espaliers, fans, cordons or pyramids. It is also worth remembering that although standard trees grow large, they can stand within or at the side of a lawn where they take up no herb or vegetable space and provide a welcome spring show of blossom as well as pleasant summer shade. It is easy to run the lawnmower underneath an apple tree. In my garden we have planted espalier apples at the end of our lawn to divide this part from the vegetable garden, and have placed a half standard quince, medlar and Ribston pippin round about for birds and blossoms to be seen from the house.

You have to be aware of the blossoming times of the apples you select to ensure pollination and a good set of fruit. Our Sturmer pippin and Ribston pippin, for example, come into blossom at more or less the same time. Though the James Grieve is usually a little later than the others the seasons will probably overlap, and pollination will be possible between the three. The Ribston pippin is one of those apples known as a triploid, which means that it needs two pollinators. Belle de Boskoop and Bramley Seedling also fall into this category, so you have to be careful to choose at least two other trees in the same flowering group when planting these. You may be lucky in having other suitable apple trees over the fence in a neighbour's garden, or in orchards nearby, but it is still wise to ensure pollination between the trees in your own garden since you can't be certain of what will happen to your neighbours' trees. All the good catalogues and fruit gardening books (including the Royal Horticultural Society's *Fruit*) show both flowering and fruiting periods. Don't be put off if you find some of them disagree. Neither apples nor people are mechanically exact, and some gardeners might consider a marginal case to fit into, say, the early flowering group, while another would put it with mid-season blossomers. Make your decision on a spread of advice from books, catalogues, a local nurseryman and people in the neighbourhood who grow apples and know how they behave in your region.

There is a greater range of apple varieties normally available in shops than of most other fruit. In my area, apart from the ubiquitous Golden Delicious, the popular Cox's orange pippin, and Bramley as the cooker, there are usually George Cave, Sturmer Pippin, Newton Wonder, Red Delicious, Worcester Pearmain, Discovery and, at Christmas, Russets. Many of them are imported, and if you are particularly fond of one of these varieties, say Cox's orange, it is certainly worth growing it for yourself, for there is all the difference in the world between a home-grown apple picked from the tree when just exactly ripe, and the same kind bought from a commercial grower which has been stored and ripened under a gas tent and then spent some time on its way to the retailer.

On the whole, though, I personally feel that if you have only a limited space, it is best to grow the old varieties, the special apples you would never ordinarily be able to have. People who do this do a service to humankind, for although apples are long-lived and there are still old trees of many kinds, all of these will die sooner or later. While commercial growers are concentrating on fewer and fewer species (and usually not the best-tasting) it is up to the private fruit gardener to keep alive the historic varieties and to demonstrate to others that apples can be delicious in more than just name.

The poor taste of a commercially-bought apple against a home-grown one of the same variety owes as much to premature picking as to the conditions under which it is stored. Every apple has its season and if you eat a Cox's orange too early, or a James Grieve too late, you will sample them at considerably less than their best. Apple literature and gardening catalogues always note the period at which each variety comes to ripening. Individual gardeners watch and taste to find the time when the apples of a particular tree in a particular year are at their very best. It is well worth the small effort.

Apples for all Seasons

As for choosing which varieties to grow, there is a vast range of possibilities. There are crisp apples which sparkle as you bite, their taste between fresh and sweet; there are heavy, creamy, musky russets; there are aromatic, spicy apples; there are innocently sweet apples with a pink tinge spreading into their flesh from their brilliantly red, waxy skins. Some should be eaten at once; others will keep for months, in some cases, years. Even quite a small garden can provide home-grown apples to eat almost the whole year round.

> I will give you . . . the names of as many [apples] with their fashions, as have come to my knowledge, either by sight or relation: for I do confesse I have not seene all that I here set down, but use the helpe of some friends.

Taking my cue from John Parkinson, I have augmented my own experience with that of other gardeners and of gardening writers, in order to make a round-the-year selection of old apples, all of them available, all but one of them at least a hundred years old, and some of them very much older.

The season begins in the middle of July with the early apples, some of which can be eaten straight from the tree. These include the Gladstone, which was rechristened with this name in 1883, having started life in the 1780s as Jackson's Seedling. Its yellow skin ripens to a deep, bright red which sets off the greenish-white flesh, and it has a pleasant, slightly winey taste. Another summer apple is the fresh-flavoured White Transparent, tender and full of juice, which takes its name from the transparence of its flesh and which originated in Russia or the Balkans, reaching Europe early in the nineteenth century. Then comes the Irish Peach, strongly recommended by Edward Bunyard as 'the queen of the early ripeners'. It is thought to have been first grown in County Sligo and was brought to England in 1820: a pale, speckled, aromatic apple, tender, white-fleshed and refreshing, which was quickly appreciated.

From mid-August we can enjoy the Lady Sudeley, raised in a Sussex cottage garden in about 1849, introduced by Bunyard, and according to him 'an apple which every garden should possess if only for its flaming fruits'. It is tender and juicy, and at its best its highly aromatic taste matches its beauty, but the tree requires good soil conditions to reach its full potential. Bunyard suggests that this variety should be gathered 'before it is willing', stored in the fruit room for a week or two and sampled from day to day until the exact moment of perfection is reached.

For September there is the excellent James Grieve, the most recently-introduced of this selection. Only rarely does a good eating apple emerge from a cross between a cooking and a dessert apple, but this descendant of Potts Seedling and Cox's orange pippin is soft, creamy, sweet and delicately handsome in its pale yellow and red.

A superb October apple is Gravenstein, thought to have arrived from Denmark in 1669. I defer to Edward Bunyard's description:

Of Gravenstein it is hard to speak in mere prose, so distinct in flavour is it, Cox itself not standing more solitary, so full of juice and scented with the very attar of apple. This aroma comes out of the oily skin and remains on the fingers despite many washings, bringing to mind the autumnal orchard in mellow sunlight.

Another October treat is the golden-brown Egremont russet (the russet most often on sale commercially) with its distinctive aromatic flavour. The Egremont has a nutty dryness to it, although the apple has plenty of juice. Less well-known but worth seeking out is the St Edmunds Pippin, an early golden russet.

Bringing us into November are the Ribston Pippin and the beloved Cox's orange pippin. For the end of the year there is Margil, a beautiful little apple known before 1750. It is one of those orange-skinned apples with russet patches, and is delicious both to taste and smell.

At its excellent best from the turn of the year through to March is the Orleans Reinette, which found its way to England a considerable time after it was first described in 1776. It is another beauty, gold flushed with red and fine russet, and like the Ribston Pippin, it is particularly rich in Vitamin C. Bunyard, who first came across it in a consignment of Blenheim Orange which he had been sent, hailed it as 'the best apple grown in western Europe'. He suggests that those who prefer their wine dry will find the Orleans Reinette to their taste, and recommends it as an accompaniment to port.

A russet for the cold, wintry months of the New Year is the Rosemary russet, first described in 1831 but of earlier origin. The Sturmer pippin is another fine late apple also recorded first in 1831. It needs a good summer to bring it to perfection, and should be left on the tree as long as possible. I have picked it from a tree bare of leaves but heavy with fruit, well into the New Year.

An apple at its best at the time when celandines, violets and hazel come into bloom, is the Cornish Gilliflower. This is not the original apple mentioned by Parkinson and Evelyn, but another which was given the same name, discovered in a Truro garden at the beginning of the nineteenth century.

The most famous of all the late-keeping apples is the French crab. It is a hard, heavy apple which is a deep clear green when picked, the side towards the sun marked with crimson like a livid bruise. As the French crab ages it turns first yellow, and then pale orange – according to George Lindley, who in 1822 ate fruit picked in 1820 and found it perfectly sound and firm. One of the French crab's alternative names is Apple-John, and it is also called the Two Years Apple, Amiens Longkeeper and Youngs Long Keeping, and other names indicative of its keeping qualities. The name 'French crab' is first encountered in the late 1700s. Well before that, in the sixteenth century, there was an apple so famed for keeping two years that the fact became built-in to its name: 'the Deux-ans or John' according

Lane's Prince Albert

D' Arcy Spice

French Crab

Ribston Pippin

Wheelers Russet

Pomme D'Api

Court Pendu Plat

to Evelyn or 'the Deusan or apple Iohn' of Parkinson; these names were further scrambled by the anonymous N.F. in *The Fruiterer's Secrets*, who wrote 'John-Apples be in some places called Dewsings or long-lasters'. Perhaps the French crab acquired its alternative names because it had the same keeping qualities as the historic AppleJohn, but it seems at least possible that they are one and the same.

Shakespeare knew these long-keeping apples. In *Henry IV, Part II*, Sir John Falstaff compares himself to one: 'Why my skin hangs about me like an old lady's loose gown: I am wither'd like an old apple-John,' and earlier, Prince Hal has made play on Sir Johns and apple-johns. In the old nursery rhyme 'I saw a ship a-sailing', the provisions include 'comfits in the cabin, And apples in the hold'. Long-keeping apples such as Apple Johns would be chosen for long voyages and in the late sixteenth century Richard Hakluyt, in a note to a trading captain, specified that amongst the food to be taken on board for the 'bankettin on shipboard of persons of credite' was 'the apple John, that dureth two yeeres, to make shew of our fruits'.

Apples at Table

Once the notion of a standard, all-purpose apple has been disposed of and one is thinking in terms of selecting apples for their variety of flavours and other qualities, one is led to think of the different ways in which they may be cooked and served. Some, of course, are best at their simplest, eaten uncooked. In the past, the most beautiful of dessert apples were brought to table and appreciated for their shape and colour as well as for their taste. Shakespeare has made us familiar with the idea of using roast apples to warm ale and wine. For a thorough review of some of the past ways of cooking and presenting apples we cannot do better than to turn to John Parkinson once more.

> The best sorts of Apples serve at the last course for the table, in most mens houses of account, where, if there grow any rare or excellent fruit, it is then set forth to be seene and tasted.
>
> Divers other sorts serve to bake, either for the Masters Table, or the meynes sustenance, either in pyes or pans, or else stewed in dishes with Rosewater and Sugar, and Cinamon or Ginger cast upon.

Some kinds are fittest to roast in the winter time, to warme a cup of wine, ale or beere; or to be eaten alone, for the nature of some fruit is never so good, or worth the eating, as when they are roasted.

Some sorts are fittest to scald for Codlings and are taken to coole the stomacke, as well as to please the taste, having Rosewater and Sugar put to them.

Some sorts are best to make Cider of, as in the West Countrey of England great quantities, yea many Hogsheads and Tunnes full are made, especially to bee carried to Sea in long voyages, and is found by experience to be of excellent use, to mixe with water for beverage. It is usually seene that those fruits that are neither fit to eat raw, roasted, nor baked, are fittest for Cider, and make the best.

The juice of Apples likewise, as of pippins, and pearemaines, is of very good use in Melancholicke diseases, helping to procure mirth, and to expell heavinesse.

The distilled water of the same Apples is of the like effect.

Gerard also mentions that sweet apples are good for 'the tempering of melancholy humours' and Bartholemew the Englishman in his encyclopaedic *De Proprietatibus Rerum,* incorporates this effect into his description of apples: 'some right sweet with a good savour and merry'.

Ancestral Apples

Examination of remains found in Neolithic sites has shown that apples were part of the diet of Neolithic people, and that some of those apples were larger than wild crab apples generally are. The evidence of Neolithic and Bronze-Age trackways suggests that early people practised a kind of tree management and were coppicing woodland for poles. Perhaps the earliest forms of apple culture in Britain were also initiated in this period. The word apple itself is of very ancient origin and occurs in the earliest written records. The three volumes of the *Leechbook of Bald* (circa 900) contain many references to apples on their own and as elements in herbal remedies. It seems likely that they were eaten in considerable quantities for their own sakes as well as in medicines, since the *Leechbook* has a remedy for 'a windy distention of the milt from eating of apples and nuts'. Apple trees are easily recognizable and long-lived and they are recorded in a number of Anglo-Saxon charters as boundary trees.

The Benedictine monks accorded considerable importance to their apples. One of the specific tasks of the monastic gardener at Westminster was to supply the brethren with apples during Advent and Lent. Orchards were highly prized, although if they were situated outside the town or castle walls, they were extremely vulnerable to attack.

There is a rhyming chronicle dating from the last quarter of the twelfth century which tells of the seige of Carlisle in the battle between Henry II and the Scottish William the Lion. This is the version quoted by Alicia Amherst:

> *They did not lose within, I assure you I do not lie*
> *As much as amounted to a single denier.*
> *But they lost their fields, with all their corn*
> *(And) their gardens (were) ravaged by those bad people,*
> *And he who could not do any more injury took it into his head*
> *To bark the apple trees! — it was a bad vengeance.*

In later times there are records of heavy fines being imposed upon those who damaged trees, particularly fruit trees, and during Henry VIII's reign, it was made illegal to bark apple, pear and other fruit trees.

The Oldest Varieties

Several varieties of apple were mentioned by name in early documents. The Pearmain is thought to be the first for which there is a written reference. However, the issue is complicated by the fact that there used also to be a Pearmain pear and one reference often cited for the apple, from a Treasury Roll of Edward I's time, actually says *'pira parmenorum'* so must surely relate to pears. However, Muriel Smith notes in the Apple Register that there were references to Pearmain apples in both England and France in about 1200, and thinks it possible that an apple grown at the National Fruit Trials, known as Old Pearmain, might be this same variety.

Another Account of Edward I (1292) has details of Costard apples, the large-ribbed apples which gave us the *costard-monger*, a seller of Costard apples, later of any apples, eventually generalized to *costermonger*, a person who sells pretty well anything from a street barrow. A number of apple names found their way into common speech and literature. Uses of 'costard' as slang for 'head' occur in Balgrove in 1530, as they do in Udall's *Ralph Roister Doister* ('I will rappe you on the costard if you playe the knave') and in Shakespeare's *King Lear* and *Richard III*. Centuries later Walter Scott, in *Rob Roy*, gave it the same meaning, but he was probably doing so as a deliberate archaism.

The apple called Bittersweet was an obvious candidate for metaphor and was used as such by Chaucer, and also by 'moral Gower' in a severe lesson:

> *Lich unto the bitter swete,*
> *For though it thenke a man first swete*
> *He shall well felen ate laste*
> *That it is sour.*

Lydgate has a passing reference to a large juicy apple known as the Pomewater, which occurs again in *Love's Labours Lost*: 'ripe as a Pomewater', and somewhat pedantically in W. Smith's *Puritan* of 1607: 'the Pomwater of his eye'! The Bittersweet has vanished, but the Pomewater as described by Parkinson in 1629 was still in existence at the end of the nineteenth century and may exist still.

The early codlings described by Parkinson and Evelyn, with their elongated, tapering shapes and highly-praised taste, are thought not to be the same as our present-day Kentish codling and Keswick codling (traced back only to 1891 and 1793 respectively). The word itself is of obscure origin, its first known occurrence in about 1440 being 'querdlynge', a spelling which continued up to Francis Bacon's time and beyond. It is believed that only incidentally, and at a fairly late date, did it become identified with a particular apple that was specially suitable for coddling, or cooking whole in a very slow and gentle way. (The verb 'to coddle' did not appear until the end of the sixteenth century.) In Worlidge's *Cyder* the codling apple is described as being 'so called from the use it is put unto, a very necessary apple in the Kitchen'. The name codlin or codling seems to have been applied to certain sorts of sour apple and other sweet kinds were given the same name when they were picked and used before they were ripe (perhaps these were thinnings). In *Twelfth Night* Shakespeare refers to 'a codling when 'tis almost an apple'; and a recipe for 1655 instructs 'Take your Pippins green and quoddle them in faire water'.

These apples, gently cooked until they were soft all through, were popular enough to be sold on the streets and a rhyme collected in 1805 runs 'A little old woman, her living she got / By selling hot codlings, hot, hot, hot.' Eliza Acton has a recipe for a tart 'of Very Young Green Apples' which seems to be a version of a coddling tart: the apples are picked 'before the cores are formed' and are baked slowly in sugar until tender quite through, when they are 'found to be *very* good'. Parkinson described codlings served with rosewater and sugar, Somerville in *Hobbinol* (1740) tempts us with 'Green Codlins' which 'float in dulcet Creams', and Swift strains our credulity with 'A codling e'er it went his lip in / Would strait become a golden Pippin'.

There are still stocks which bear the name of Golden pippin but these are probably not the true old variety. It would be difficult for any apple to live up to the descriptions given of the Golden pippin from the beginning of the seventeenth century onwards. Forsyth in 1831 is lyrical about its favours and he notes also that there are several kinds.

> The Golden Pippin is well known; and the French own it to be of English origin. It is almost peculiar to England; for there are few countries abroad where it succeeds well. It is yellow as gold; the juice is very sweet; the skin (especially when exposed to the sun) is often freckled with dark yellow spots. It is certainly the most antient as well as the most excellent Apple that we have. It ripens in October, and will keep through the winter. There are several varieties of this fruit.

In the earliest references, pippins are often paired with 'Blaundrelles', as in John Russell's account of seasonal fare written in about 1460. The Household Ordnances of Edward IV describe 'Pourveyours of blaundrelles, pepyns and all other fruytes'. Cotgrave describes a 'Blandureau, the white apple, called in some parts of England a blaundrell', and this gives us a clue to its modern identity. Blandureau is an alternative name for a white apple known better as Calville Blanc d'Hiver, which is at the National Fruit Trials and in many other collections. Purveyors of pippins like those mentioned in the Ordnances were known as 'Pippin-mongers'; a usage which, unlike 'Costard-monger', has no modern form. Weelkes's part-song based on street cries refers to 'hot pippin pies'. Another such cry was for 'hot pippins piping hot', which may have been coddled or baked.

In a play from the mid-eighteenth century called *The London Chanticleers*, in which the characters are named after their trades, 'Jenniting, an apple wench' sells a selection of apples: 'Come buy me pearmains, curious John Apples, dainty pippins. Come who buy? Who buy?' Geneting apples, thought to be English in origin, were known from at least 1600 and are said to have taken their name from the time when they ripened, around St John's day. This cannot have been the apostle John, for his feast day is in December and the Geneting is an early season apple. Cotgrave writes (1655) of 'S. John's apple, a kind of soone ripe sweeting'. Of the sixty or more St Johns, John Fisher, Bishop of Rochester, who was martyred in 1535, is the only English saint with a special significance for this period and a feast day in June. Among the other seasonal names for the Geneting are: May pippin, Yellow May pippin and a June-eating, a rationalized version of their original name. The *Apple Register* notes that the Geneting or Joaneting, 'a small ribbed yellow apple, occasionally tinted orange', was in existence in 1920, and it may still be so.

Of all the pippin apples, the Ribston pippin is probably the best known. It found its way into *Pickwick Papers* – 'a little hard-headed Ribston-pippin faced man' – and even into an odd little poem by Hilaire Belloc which alludes to its hearty quality. The Ribston, Cox's orange, Sturmer, St Edmunds (also known as the St Edmunds Russet), Wyken, King of Pippins and countless more apples have the word pippin in their names. It is not, in fact, a precise term, and its derivation is uncertain. It has been explained in various ways, none of which is entirely convincing: an apple originally grown from seed, or one which looks like an apple grown from seed, or one which has many pips, or one which has small spots or 'pips' on its skin. The one characteristic pippins do seem to have in common is that they are all dessert apples. In *Euphues* (1579), Lyly drew a contrast between the 'sour Crabbe' and the 'sweet pippin', and this distinction continues to hold true.

It is still possible to buy the King of the Pippins, which was first recorded in about 1800 and which has its own nursery rhyme:

> *Little King Pippin*
> *He built a fine hall,*
> *Pie crust and pastry crust*
> *That was the wall;*

The windows were made
Of black pudding and white,
And slated with pancakes,
You ne'er saw the like.

The King of the Pippins is also sometimes called the Queen of the Pippins, but the most famous Queen apple was of a quite different identity. It originated in the sixteenth century and was renowned for its beauty and flavour. Ben Jonson made a somewhat obscure reference to it: 'Only your nose inclines / That side that's next the sun to the queene apple', but the meaning is made clear by Forsyth's description of the apple: 'a beautiful fruit, red towards the sun and a fine yellow on the other side'. He thought it 'a very fine apple', second only to the Golden Pippin.

Cider Apples

Many of the apples grown in the past went to make cider or verjuice. They were for the most part special sour-tasting varieties (although John Evelyn has notes on cider-making from Pippins and Winter Pearmains). Even modern varieties of cider apple are quite difficult to obtain and the old names of the seventeenth century such as Genet Moyle and Bromebury Crab seem to have disappeared entirely.

There is still a Somerset Red Streak available but I do not know whether it is related to the ancient Red Streaks. A variety which has been known for nearly a hundred years is the Crimson King, another Somerset apple, sold by Scotts in Somerset, one of only a handful of nurseries to advertise cider apples.

CHAPTER SIX

The Variety of Pears

IT IS MORE DIFFICULT to detect pears at their finest moment than to do likewise for apples. Lydgate's passing reference which warns 'Appeles and peres that semen gode, / Full ofte tyme are roten by the core' is far more true of pears than of apples. Sir Thomas Browne even went so far as to make a simile of 'as rotten as a Pear'. Taken too early, pears are dry and unyielding, too late, and they are sleepy and tasteless. Never having been a pear zealot, the subtleties described by the cognoscenti have until recently been a mystery closed to me. Why should John Parkinson feel required to expatiate upon pears to the extent of describing no less than sixty-seven kinds, exceeding even his chapter on apples? Why were such great quantities of pears, many specified by name, sent to kings and their courts as they travelled abroad in the early Middle Ages? Why did Edward Bunyard, early this century, ransack the language for ecstatic prose to describe his favourite pear kinds?

There was an occasion during the time I was working on this book which gave me some inkling of what a pear could be. On a bitter November day, the worse for coming abruptly on the heels of a period of mild and glowing autumn weather, I was passing through a pear orchard on the way to look at some old apple trees and I idly picked up a windfall pear – there were plenty of them that day. It was not easy to ignore the cold and the rough wind which had just started to carry the first sleety snow of winter, but that tender, honeyed pear, just slightly musky and with a suggestion of sharpness in it, drew complete concentration of mind and senses into its appreciation. It was a mixture of tastes rather than one precise flavour, and delicious beyond imagination.

I suspect that with pears, rather more than any other fruits, you have to grow them for yourself in order to achieve such exquisiteness. The nuances of taste disappear from commercially-produced fruit long before they get to the table. The variety is also critical. Dessert pears offer a wide choice in texture and taste: from meltingly soft to relatively crisp; from heavily musky to delicately bland, sometimes with a flowery scent of roses or of cinnamon, and varying greatly in sweetness, acidity and astringency. Some pears are so generous in proportion and so running with juice as to make casual eating impossible; others are juicy but self-contained, tasting best when eaten straight from the tree. We still have a fine range of shapes and colours to choose from. There are smooth green pears, and yellows and reds, variously sprinkled or covered with freckles and russet. They come in curious round apple-like shapes and in beautiful pure ovals, as well as in the characteristic pyriform of the species with that lumpy bulge so pronounced in the well-known Williams Bon Chrétien. There are the smooth plump conical shapes of pears like Beurre Hardy, the longer, slimmer lines of Conference, the hump-shouldered shape of Bergamotte, and many other variations.

Most nurseries will offer you a choice between Williams and Conference and sometimes Comice, but there are many other varieties still available. Clearly it would be better to taste a wide range, and sample one against another to find one which exactly suits your palate, but usually this is not possible. A review of what some lovers of the pear have said can give you an idea of what to expect, though as ever, while each writer confidently decrees that this or that is 'the best pear' the varieties they choose are quite different.

To begin in familiar territory, the names that everyone knows are Williams and Conference. The Williams Bon Chrétien began life as a seedling in Aldermaston in the late eighteenth century. It grew in the garden of a schoolmaster named Wheeler, which was later taken over by another schoolmaster named Stair and named after him. Grafts of the Stair's pear were sent to Richard Williams, a nurseryman of Turnham Green, and it was renamed after him in 1814. It was taken to America at the end of the eighteenth century but it was not until 1817 that Enoch Bartlett took over land on which it was growing unnamed and rechristened it the Bartlett. In South Africa, where it is also widely grown, it is known as the Bon Chrétien.

The Williams Bon Chrétien was exhibited in the Royal Horticultural Society in 1816 and well thought-of from the first. George Lindley found the flesh 'whitish, very tender and delicate, abounding with a sweet and agreeably perfumed juice'. Hogg in 1862 believed it to be 'one of the finest of pears' and noted that it should be gathered before the pale green skin becomes yellow. Unlike some pears, it can be picked early and ripened in store: indeed it is best ripened off slowly in a cool store room. Despite its favourable reception, the Williams Bon Chrétien did not receive the Royal Horticultural Society's Award of Merit until as late as 1970. It is now one of the most widely-grown pears throughout the world, produced both for dessert and processing.

The long, russetted Conference is by comparison a newcomer. Raised in Essex by Thomas Rivers, it was exhibited in 1885 at the National Pear Conference and named after this event. Its slightly pinkish flesh is juicy and sweet, though it is not regarded by connoisseurs as in quite the first rank for taste. Both the Conference and the Williams Bon Chrétien are regular and reliable croppers with fruit which stores well, factors which have undoubtedly contributed to their ubiquity.

A pear which used to be more widely available than it is now, the Doyenne du Comice, is the most famous pear of all for its flavour. Stocks are readily available from good nurserymen so it can be grown in gardens. Unfortunately, when the fire-blight disease and its eradication campaign destroyed most of Laxton Superb, Doyenne de Comice lost its best pollinator. However, when you consider that Laxton Superb was raised as late as 1901 and Doyenne de Comice was known as far back as 1849 when it was raised at Angers sur Loire, there are obviously alternative pollinators. Of these Glou Morceau is a good choice and a fine, sweet late pear in its own right (its name said to derive from the Flemish *golou*, meaning delicious). The highest praise, however, is reserved for the Comice. Plump and greeny-yellow, speckled, flushed with red and full of juice, with a perfume of cinnamon and a meltingly refreshing taste, it is generally agreed that a Comice at its best is incomparable. Bunyard suggests that the fruits be stored in a cool fruit room or cellar and individually inspected each day until the time of perfection, which occurs when the colour changes from green to yellow under its fine russet mantle.

Though it tends to come into flower a little earlier, another fine-tasting pear which will pollinate the Doyenne du Comice is the Beurre Hardy. It is, in fact, hardy, though named not for that reason, but after a M. Hardy, director of the Luxembourg Gardens during the nineteenth century. A handsome pear, roundish, it is russet-brown in colour reddening towards the sun, with a faint scent of rosewater. It will also pollinate both the Beurre Superfin (a creamy, melting, aromatic fruit, first raised near Angers in the mid-nineteenth century), and another fine pear, the Josephine de Malines, named after the wife of Major Esperen who raised it in 1830. Unlike most pears, the Josephine de Malines will keep over a period of weeks, ripening successively in store, from December to January. Hardy by nature, it produces generous quantities of small, green fruits which ripen to a subtle yellow. The flesh is creamy-rose in colour, sweetly perfumed and rich in taste.

We mostly think of pears as dessert fruit but in the past, cooking pears were as highly regarded. Some of these are ancient varieties and are still available today from certain nurseries. The Catillac, first described in 1665 in the *Jardinier Français*, has kept its reputation as one of the finest cooking pears over three centuries. It is supposed to have been named after the place where it was first discovered, in Cadillac in the Gironde. The flesh, which is creamy-coloured and hard when raw, cooks to a deep red.

The most famous cooking pear of all was the Warden. It is mentioned by Alexander Neckham, both in *De Naturis Rerum* (written in the late twelfth century) where the Warden Pear is included among the trees and herbs chosen for a noble garden, and in his later poem *De Laudibus Divinae Sapientiae*, where *volema* (Warden) appears in a similar context. It is generally accepted that these pears, which were the most famous for roasting or baking, were first introduced by the monks of Warden Abbey in Bedfordshire. The Abbey's arms are three Warden pears, but it seems equally likely that the monks may have taken a punning coat from these ancient pears. In 1544, Fitzherbert mentions Wardens among fruits which are 'profytable and also a pleasure to a housbande'. Sir Francis Bacon includes Wardens among the fine trees in his garden essay. Indeed, Wardens were so popular that they were often mentioned separately from other pears, and it seems as if there were at least two sorts; Thomas Tusser mentions 'Wardens, red and white' in his list of fruits. The most glowing reference to Wardens comes in the poem by Robert Herrick 'To the Most Fair and Lovely Mistress Anne Soame, now Lady Abdie', in which he builds up a fragrant tribute of the most delicious odours such as 'the flower of blooming clove, / Or roses smothered in the stove', 'neat and woven bowers, / All over-arched with orange flowers' and not least among these, the 'roasted warden or baked pear'. This aroma must have lingered in

London streets as late as 1703, when there is an allusion to a melancholy street cry of 'Hot baked Wardens, and Pippins' *(The London Spy)*. Baked pears figure in many old cookery books from John Russell's *Boke of Nurture (c.* 1460) to Eliza Acton in 1845, as indeed they do in some modern ones, though in latterday recipes the variety of pear is not specified.

It is still possible to buy a pear known as the Black Worcester. This is said to have been grown in Worcester before 1575 and to be the pear on the city coat of arms. Hogg lists among its synonyms the name Parkinson's Warden, but Parkinson himself describes it only as 'like a Warden, and as good', when baked. If however, as is implied by the context of some of the old references, there were several kinds of Warden pear, it seems quite probable that the Black Worcester is one of these. It is a large, red-brown pear with rough dots on it, its flesh coarse and gritty, sharp in flavour, but with a trace of sweetness. Eliza Acton says that if Iron pears, as she calls the Black Worcester, are put to bake thoroughly in a bread oven as it cools overnight 'they will be excellent, very sweet, and juicy and much finer in flavour than those which are stewed or baked with sugar'. The Black Worcester is entirely a culinary pear and will last through until February.

Many of the early pears which were grown and relished in great quantities in the early Middle Ages are lost now to us. As well as Wardens, Alexander Neckham mentions the Pear of St Regulo, also called St Rule Pears or Regul Pears, as in a memorandum surviving from the reign of Edward I which detailed fruit sent to the king and the court. They must have been greatly enjoyed: in one Palm Sunday week, eight hundred and fifty Regul Pears were sent, and in the week of Epiphany no less than one thousand seven hundred. There are earlier references, as for instance, to the one hundred pears of 'S. Rule' sent to Henry III in 1223. It was the most-mentioned pear in the thirteenth century but by the end of the sixteenth century and the beginning of the seventeenth there is no sign of it. It is absent from Gerard, Parkinson and Evelyn, so there is no description of what it looked like or how it tasted.

Other pears delivered to Edward I were Martin, Sorell and Chyrfoll pears, Calluewell and Pase Pucell, Dieyes and Gold Knopes. Some of these may be traced three centuries later. Parkinson describes the Pucell as 'a greene peare, of an indifferent good taste' and there are two Sorells, a black and a red, against which there is nothing said, although there is no praise either. Another pear mentioned late in Henry III's reign was the Janettar. It may be this pear tree which is the site of action for the last part of Chaucer's *Merchant's Tale*, where May, the young wife, is first described as

> *... ful more blisful on to see*
> *Than is the newe pere-jonette tree;*

It is a very forward tree, as Chaucer was probably aware, and his Lady May is also forward, not to say ingenious, as her remarkable arboreal infidelity later proves. In Piers Plowman, 'pere Ionettes' are also mentioned in passing. Parkinson appears to swap the elements of the name around, and calls this pear the Geneting pear, describing it as 'a very good early ripe pear'. Whether these pears were synonymous or not is a matter of conjecture; there are only the names to judge by since no physical trace now remains of Janettar, Ionettes or Geneting.

The same is true of the Catherine or Katherine pear. Like Ben Jonson's Queen apple, it was famous for its blush, and is best remembered from Sir John Suckling's poem 'A Ballad upon a Wedding' (1641).

> *Her cheek so rare a white was on,*
> *No daisy makes comparison;*
> *Who sees them is undone;*
> *For streaks of red were mingled there,*
> *Such as are on a Catherine pear,*
> *The side that's next the sun.*

Parkinson says plainly that 'The Catherine peare is knowne to all I thinke to be a yellow red sided peare, of a full waterish sweete taste, and ripe with the foremost', and Evelyn casts it with his recommended varieties. John Gay returns to the theme in *Pastorals* (1650), with 'Catherine pears adorn my ruddy cheek', but it is very much later that we find George Crabbe, in 1819, writing 'Twas not the lighter red, that partly streaks the Catherine pear, that brightened o'er her cheeks'. The Catherine pear seems to have disappeared from the fruit gardening books at some time in the early nineteenth century. Lindley has no mention of it in his list of one hundred and sixty-two pears (1831), nor has Hogg later that century. However, in 1817, Brookshaw was certainly acquainted with the Catherine pear, although unenthusiastic about its qualities: 'sweet and juicy, with a degree of musky flavour: but at best is considered a common pear'. Maybe it was always more renowned for its beauty than for surpassing flavour. In past times it must have been a useful early pear, pleasant, if not of first excellence and by Austen's account (1653) a reliable cropper: 'but for constant bearing kind I know none better than the Catherine peare'. During the nineteenth century new early season pears were bred and discovered, the comely Catherine fell out of favour and gradually reached the point of extinction.

The pear reputed to be the oldest variety of all, and to have been brought to Britain by the Romans, is the Autumn Bergamot. The earliest written reference to be traced is, however, in Switzerland in the early eighteenth century. There are still specimens of this pear (though it is not commercially for sale) but the nomenclature is confusing since it is often marked as synonymous with the French *Bergamotte d'Automne* and with the English Bergamot, although there is every evidence that these are distinctly different varieties. Muriel Smith of the National Fruit Trials described the Autumn Bergamot as a yellowish-green pear ripening about mid-October, with an occasional flush and with a variable amount of rough russet: coarse, gritty, sweet and juicy in taste. This agrees quite well with earlier authorities such as George Lindley (1831) and Hogg (1862), though Lindley finds it gritty only near the core and remarks particularly on its 'richly perfumed juice', adding that 'It is one of the best pears of the season'. Hogg calls it a 'fine old dessert pear', noting also that 'it is a vigorous grower, hardy, forms a handsome standard, and is a most abundant bearer'.

There is a pear called Summer Rose which is also recommended highly by George Lindley as 'a most excellent and beautiful variety'. It is unusual, having a rounded shape more like an apple than a pear, and it is a beauty with 'skin inclining to yellow, speckled with russet; but of a bright rich red, intermingled with brown spots on the sunny side'. Hogg notes that the flesh is crisp, though sweet and juicy. It was also known as Thorny Rose, Poire de Rose and Caillot Rosat, and Bunyard believes it might be the 'Cailleau' mentioned in the original version of the *Roman de la Rose* by Jehan de Meung and Gillaume de Loris and so-called because it was small and flattened in shape like a pebble or *caillou*. If this is so, it is also the same pear as the Calluewell and Calwell pears we meet with in the various English accounts of the thirteenth century.

A dessert pear which was well-known before 1600 and is still available from certain nurseries is the Jargonelle. As you might guess from the name this variety is thought to have originated in France, but it has since acquired the synonym of English Jargonelle (the pear known in France as Jargonelle is now quite distinct). This green and brown summer fruit has a creamy flesh which is tender and juicy, with a musky piquancy from which a strong essence can be made. The flavour of pear drops is that of the Jargonelle. It is a hardy pear and will succeed well in less sunny districts and as far north as Scotland.

We have an insight into some of the old gardens of the past, not only through household accounts and inventories, but sometimes more intimately through diaries and notebooks. These entries from a seventeenth-century journal kept by Henry Osenden of Barham, Kent, show a zeal and generosity in the pursuit of gardening which can still be found today though usually in more limited circumstances.

Feb. 11, 1635   set the hawksbill pares in the garden in Maydeken. planted the cherry garden at Great Maydeken.

Feb. 14, 1652   gave Mr Barling 4 apple trees and a peare tree, viz. a musk pare tree.

Feb. 10, 1652   sent my coz Henry Oxinden the yew tree . . . lent him then my stone rowle.

Nov. 16, 1647   planted twentie-five peare trees in the garden that is walled about at Great Maydeken. . . .

Nov. 1654   took up out of the nursery at Maydeken 1 quince tree, 2 warden trees and 3 other peare trees, and set ym in Byton, and 1 pear tree against the bake house windore, I allso sete one medlar tree and a nutmeg peach tree in the garden.

Feb. 19, 1655   grafted one of the best pares Capt. Meriwether hath uppon a tree beside the house at South Barham; made a crosse upon it: it is to be eaten in Feb.

1639   hee (Sir Basil Dexivell at Boome) planted his orchard agt. his back dore agt. the Hall.

Feb. 7, 1647   Lieutenant Hobdat planted 10 apple trees, in his orchard next his garden, which I gave him.

Mr Osenden seems to have been a man with a continuing fondness for pears, since he planted many of them and over a long period.

All the named varieties are in Parkinson's list. The Hawkesbill was of 'middle size and like the Rowling Pear, and not good before it be a little rowled or bruised, to make it eate the more mellow'. The Muske Peare was similar to the Catherine in size, colour and form but 'farre more excellent in taste'. We cannot say what Captain Meriwether's 'best pare' was, but it is interesting to see what a free exchange of fruit trees there was in these times.

Pears were generally held in greater favour in past times than they are now. Gerard (1597) writes of peares 'which to describe apart, were to send an owle to Athens, or to number those things which are without number'. Ralph Austen (1653) quotes 'a late author' persuaded that in the mid-seventeenth century there were four to five hundred 'several kinds of Pears'.

Perry was a popular drink then, and a number of varieties were grown especially for this purpose. The Red pear, mentioned by John Evelyn, and several pears listed by Hogg a century ago, are still available, among them the Blakeney Red, Butt, Thorn, Winnals London and Yellow Huffcap.

All of the pear varieties are believed to derive originally from the Wild pear, *Pyrus communis*, known as a 'doubtful native' in Britain, although Oliver Rackham, our best authority on native trees, believes it to be indigenous to this island. It is a beautiful tree, tall and upright, with white blossom in the spring. It is certain that pears were also imported in early times; the Romans were using several varieties in Pliny's time.

It seems sad that people nowadays may well be able to buy fewer varieties of pear at a fruit market than the Romans could. However, it is still possible to find stocks of many historic varieties to grow yourself. It used to be said that you 'plant pears for your heirs' because the pear is naturally slow to mature though hardy, and pears on their own roots or on pear stock may take ten or twenty years to produce fruit. However, on other stocks (principally 'Quince A' rootstock nowadays), pears may begin to fruit within a few years of planting in a good soil. But with the hope of growing trees to delight future generations, perhaps one should still take 'pears for your heirs' as a motto in a wider sense.

CHAPTER SEVEN

Plums and Bullaces, Damsons and Prunes

IT IS STILL POSSIBLE to find plums of several kinds growing wild or semi-wild in the English countryside. I remember delicious bullaces from Essex hedges, especially good because they keep their flavour when bottled or frozen and can be brought out joyfully in the long winter months for fruit pies. Bullaces grow where I live now in Hertfordshire and there are also cherry plums (known locally as melly-bellies) to be found in the hedgerows, but while I have watched these ripen, I have never tasted one because the places they grow are also well known to children and birds and they always get there first. Our local name for these is, I think, a corruption of the alternative name for cherry plum, myrobalan. Cherry plums are planted round the cider orchards in Somerset. The growth is naturally dense, and an even thicker wall of foliage is created by cutting and weaving their branches, which are unusually flexible for a plum. Another plum I have found in a semi-wild state in hedgerows is the Aylesbury prune, a wry, dark, damson-like little plum which seems never to have decided whether its career lies inside or outside orchards. It is a strong hardy tree and was in the past much planted as a windbreak as well as for its fruit.

In many counties where orchard plums are rare, plum trees are deliberately grown in hedges, their tall bushy forms providing shelter for animals, while at the same time producing an appreciable crop. Small commercial enterprises of this kind may be found on farms in Cheshire, Shropshire, Lancashire and Westmorland. The most successful plum for these conditions is the hardy damson; in many of these counties it would be the Shropshire damson (the damson prune). It was estimated in 1961 that there were as many as half a million damson trees in Britain, those recorded in Kent and

Worcestershire accounting for nearly half of this figure, but I would guess that this number has diminished over the past twenty years. Plums have become less popular as commercial fruits and hedges have been grubbed up in many counties.

The Aylesbury prune is believed to have originated as a natural seedling of the bullace known as *Prunus domestica institia*, a subspecies of the main plum species, *P. domestica*. The aggregate species *P. domestica* is itself thought to be the result of an ancient cross between the sloe, *P. spinosa*, and the cherry plum, another separate species *P. cerasifera*. *P. domestica* includes among its subspecies the bullace, the gages (ssp *italica*), and the subspecies *domestica* which includes most of the other plums, of which over a hundred and fifty kinds are known to us. There is also the little yellow Mirabelle plum which is found growing semi-wild over much of Europe, the result of a hybridization between *P. cerasifera* and *P. domestica*. This remarkable inter-fertility between species and subspecies has given rise to a vast number of plum forms.

A number of plum varieties subsequently brought under cultivation were originally discovered as natural seedlings in hedges and woodlands. These include well-known and commercially important kinds such as Victoria and Pershore plums and the Farleigh damson. The Victoria, nowadays one of the two or three plums sold regularly in shops, was found in a garden in Alderton in Sussex. It was sold to a Brixton nurseryman called Danyer, and formally introduced in 1840. It is a self-fertile plum and is the one kind sold by almost all fruit nurseries nowadays.

I chose a Victoria some years ago when I had a garden with chalky soil, not really suited for plum growing, and I found it a very willing tree. In fact, the year after I left that house it produced a wonderful mass of blossom. Greedy for plums though you may be, it is not wise to let all of a very heavy crop grow to maturity, since however hard the tree tries, over-cropping will lead to small and rather flavourless fruit. Another variety that characteristically tends to overdo things is the Early Transparent gage. With both this and the Victoria, judicious pruning of the fruits when they are tiny will put matters right. Though the Victoria is not accounted one of the best-flavoured plums by connoisseurs, it can be a very pleasant dessert plum. Most commercial crops are picked early, for use mainly in cooking (the Victoria is a dual-purpose plum), because early picking decreases the likelihood of financial loss through decay. The home orchardist can, however, afford to leave the fruit to ripen slowly on the tree until the end of August, when it will be succulent, sweet and juicy.

A chance discovery now grown commercially rather than in private gardens is the Pershore, named after its place of origin. It was found growing in Tiddesley Woods, Pershore (now in Hereford and Worcester) by Gordon Crooke in 1827. A largish, yellow plum, it is also known as Pershore Yellow Egg and Yellow Egg. It is not an eating plum but is good for cooking and processing. The Farleigh damson is also named after the place in Kent where it was found. This small, blue-black culinary wildling was introduced in 1820. While not the first choice among damsons for taste, it has a good flavour and brings forth its small dark fruits in prodigious quantities.

Plums have been cultivated for at least two thousand years in Europe and Asia, and in Britain probably since the Roman occupation and possibly before. The blackthorn or sloe *(Prunus spinosa)* is the only native plum species, but other sorts have become widely naturalized – even the greengage is known as an escape from cultivation. Among the earliest references to the plum are two entries in the Anglo-Saxon *Leechbook of Bald* of the early tenth century. In one part of the *Leechbook* there is a recommendation for a decoction of leaves as a mouthwash 'For a mouth troubled with eruption within: take leaves of a plum tree, boil in wine, and swill the mouth therewith.' In Book II 'plum fruits' to be eaten 'after a night's fasting' are recommended among other remedies for modifying the workings of the lower intestine. This reference is probably to bullace or damson-type plums (whose astringent properties were being enlisted to remedy loose bowel action only a few decades ago in France). The sweet sorts of plum tend to have the opposite effect.

The damson has been popular over many centuries. It is among the first plums to have been mentioned by name by a number of early writers. A note in Lanfrank's *Science of Cirurgie*, which dates from the fourteenth century, prescribes 'figis' and 'damascenes'. Bartholemew the Englishman, in his thirteenth-century *De Proprietatibus Rerum*, gave damsons a high commendation: 'Of plumme tree in many manere of kynde but the Damacene is the best.' Andrew Boorde's *Dyetary* of 1542 advises that 'damysens eaten before dyner, be good to provoke a man's appetyde'.

In John Russell's *Boke of Nurture* (c. 1460), a reference to 'plomys, damsons, cheries' which are to be served on a fasting

stomach shows that different kinds of plum were certainly distinguished by this date. Thomas Tusser includes several kinds of plums
in a list in the *Five Hundred Points of Good Husbandrie* (1573). These
are 'Boolesse, black and white; Damsens, white and black; and
Wheat Plums'. When William Lawson came to write his *New
Orchard and Garden* in 1618 he recommended for northern gardens
'Red and White Plums, Damsons, Bullis'.

There were 'ploumes' and 'bolas' in the beautiful garden of
Chaucer's *Romaunt of the Rose* (about 1369), but Lawson recommends that 'Plums, Damsons and Bulless' along with filberts 'be
removed from the plain soyl of your Orchard into your fence: for
there is not such fertility and easeful growth, as within, and there
also they are more subject to, and can abide the blast of Aeolus'. He
observes also that planted in this fashion they act as a kind of shelter-
belt for the fruits inside the orchard, which generally speaking
mature later, and would be more likely in any case to be damaged by
the winds. It is clear however, that he considers the fruit trees
placed within the orchard to be 'your better fruit', perhaps because
the plums had a harder struggle to sweet maturity in the more
northern parts of the country.

Certainly in the south they were a popular fruit. Samuel Hartlib,
a Pole who settled in England in about 1628, noted that 'in Kent
and Surrey, plums pay no small part of the rent'. Plums were recorded among the presents of fruit made to Henry VIII, and when
his flagship the *Mary Rose*, which sank in the Solent in 1545, was
investigated and examined after nearly four and a half centuries,
plums, probably damsons, were found among the provisions.

Parkinson lists a good selection of plums. He also makes special
mention of the large size and vigorous growth of plum trees, the
features which led Lawson to consider them best grown on the
periphery of the orchard, where the poorer soil would modify their
growth, though, even so, they would naturally grow big enough to
provide good breaks against the wind. Parkinson also notes that
plums were imported, dried as prunes, from France. The great
Damaske plums when dried were sold in grocers' shops as Damask
prunes. Bullaces were also dried and these were sold as 'French
Prunes'.

It seems that prunes have always been mostly imported, though
we can tell from old recipes and recommendations for drying that
country housewives used also to make their own. There is no clear

reason why an imported prune should be preferred to an English one. Experiments in drying plums, conducted when there was a glut of them after the Second World War, showed dried English plums to be of very good quality. There is, however, a strong tradition that the imported ones are superior, and indeed the descriptions from the past do sound attractive. This is from *The Child's Guide to Knowledge*, two hundred and fifty years later than Parkinson:

Q What are Prunes?
A French Plums dried; they are usually very prettily packed
   in boxes and exported from France.
Q Whence do they principally come?
A From Brignolles, a town of Provence about thirty miles from
   Marseilles; this is one of the most famous places in France
   for dried plums; also from Bourdeaux, a rich town in Guienne.

It is interesting to find Hogg only a few years later recommending particular varieties for home drying. These are plump plums, rich in sugars, which give a good meaty prune when dried. Hogg clearly felt that one did not necessarily have to look to France for a 'Prune of Brignole' but that it was enough simply to procure the right variety.

D'Agen if dried forms the famous Prune d'Agen; Blue Perdrigon when dried forms the Prunes of Brignole; Ickworth Imperatrice is an excellent drying plum; St Catherine is esteemed for drying; St Julien does well for drying.

I have a very good recipe for Christmas pudding which includes prunes among the ingredients, but prunes were not in fact the fruit in the old 'plum puddings' served at Christmas time. A nineteenth-century writer, Stephen Dowell, explains it clearly: 'The dried grapes ... we term simply raisins when used for eating uncooked, and plums when they form an ingredient in the famous English plum pudding'. It is thought that in some early recipe, perhaps for 'plum broth', raisins were substituted for the plums, though the original term was retained, and that the usage stuck. This seems to have happened well before the seventeenth century ended, for a humorous reference dating from 1660 clearly indicates raisins in the famous dish:

... but there is your Christmas pye and that hath plums in abundance. . . .
He that discovered the new star in Cassiopeia . . . deserves not half so much
to be remembered as he that first married mince-meat and Raisins together.

So when Little Jack Horner, whose rhyme dates from the sixteenth
century, 'Stuck in his thumb', what he pulled out was in fact a
raisin, and they are raisins too, and not squashy plums, in the little
rhyme 'Clap hands, Daddy comes, With his pockets full of Plums,
And a cake for little Alice.'

The bullace is probably the most ancient English plum, discount-
ing the sloe (which although it had an important part in plum genetics is not in common usage considered a plum). There is a long,
continuous history of bullaces in hedgerows. Even before Chaucer's
Romaunt, they are mentioned in the mid-fourteenth-century
romance, *William and the Werwolf*: 'bolaces & blakeberies that on
breres growen'. Gerard notes that 'the wilde Plums', that is bullaces
and sloes, 'grow in most hedges through England'. In Smollett's
Sir Lancelot Graves is a passing reference to bullaces being gathered
along with haws.

It is accepted that the name 'damson' comes from 'damascene',
but early sources mention both names in such a way as to suggest
that people then used damson and damascene for distinctly different
sorts of plum. In the late sixteenth century, when Gerard mentions
a few of the many plums available (he himself had 'three score sorts
in my garden and all strange and rare'), two of his main groups are
the common damson and the 'Damascen Plum'. Evelyn lists
'Damson: white and black', 'Damasq' and 'Damazene'. Hogg's
nineteenth-century choice gives no less than eleven 'damas' names
and one 'Damaseen', as well as several damsons.

There are a number of old recipes for using damsons. Unlike
other culinary plums, damsons are high in sugars, but they are also
highly astringent. This gives them their own particular, agreeable
flavour, but for most tastes, makes them too sharp to be eaten raw.
Personally, I enjoy a few ripe damsons from the tree, but in quantity
I would join the crowd and make stewed damsons or damson pie.
('Damson' or 'damson pie' was used in the nineteenth century as
slang for bad language – presumably because of the similarity between 'damson' and 'damns' – as in Black's *Strange Adventure of a
Phaeton*: 'Even if you were to hear some of the Bingham lads giving
each other a dose of damson-pie . . . you wouldn't understand a

single sentence.') Damson gin, which tastes something like sloe gin, used to be popular; but most famous of all were the brilliant clear damson jellies and crusty sugared damson cheese. Dorothy Hartley recalls longingly the Yorkshire tables on which appeared 'damson cheese, crimson in a pool of port wine on a gold-washed dish'. She rates a well-made damson cheese very highly and tells of an old way of serving it which would probably be excessive for a modern table, but which can be fully enjoyed in description.

> The cheeses were sometimes poured out on to deep old dinner plates and after some days in a dry store cupboard, were turned out and stacked one atop the other with spice and bay leaves between, and the whole pile covered over from dust and kept in the warm dry cupboard till shrunk and crusty with candied sugar. Such old damson cheese was a foot high, a foot across, and quite hard.

Opinion on the merits of the various kinds of plum is, as always, divided. Two plums on Evelyn's recommended list of 'excellent Fruit-Trees', the Primoridian (or Primordial) and the Date plum, are counted by Parkinson as 'no very good Plum' and 'of a waterish taste, not pleasing'. On the other hand, they agree on the merits of the Nutmeg plum, 'no bigger than a Damson ... of a greenish yellow colour when it is ripe ... with us about Bartholemew tide, and is a very good plum', and of the 'well-relished' Perdigon (or Perdrigon), an early blackish 'dainty good plumme'. This plum is also praised by Batty Langley and Philip Miller, and is the one mentioned by Hakluyt in 1582: 'Of late time the Plum called the *Perdegevena*, was procured out of Italy, with two kinds more, by the Lord Cromwell, after his travell'. Hogg recommends it as 'a good old plum, suitable either for the dessert or preserving'. He goes on to warn that since 'the bloom is very tender and susceptible of early spring frosts' it requires to be grown against an east or a south-east wall, which may be a reason for its failure at the National Fruit Trials, where it never cropped satisfactorily and was grubbed up in 1976. Stock went to the National Fruit Trials from two English nurseries at the beginning of this century, and from the Netherlands as late as 1955, so it is possible that there are still old trees of this ancient variety in existence and perhaps still yielding the deep purple plums of early renown, with succulent yellow flesh, full of excellent juice, which falls away from the stone.

The Myrobalan is also mentioned in early records. Gerard praises it, though he notes that it was in the habit then, as now, of bringing forth fruit only 'every other yeare'. It has been much used as a rootstock, but this little plum can be enjoyed for its own sake. H. V. Taylor was well aware of its beauty and excellence:

> These shrubs or trees are very handsome for the leaves are a beautiful glossy green, and the pure white three-quarter inch flowers are produced in great abundance. The flowering shoots are so beautiful and produced so early in the season as to attract attention and the shrub has become a florist flower. Flowering branches are occasionally seen on sale in florist's shops during March and April. . . . The little fruits are soft, juicy, sweet and pleasantly flavoured . . . coming to maturity in July, when no other plums are available, they readily sell, and in the hands of good chefs make delectable pies and stewed dishes.

Taylor wrote his plum classic in 1948, and I am sorry to say that nowadays cherry plums for sale at mid-summer, or indeed at any time, would be a rarity. I have never seen these fruits for sale, though I thought I had come near to it once when I noticed 'Myrobalan plums' on a menu as an accompaniment for a fish dish. When I questioned the chef, however, he produced a jar of 'Héro' plums, bottled in France, which was what he made his sauce with. As with so many other fruit varieties, the answer seems to be that if you want to try these old flavours, you must grow the trees for yourself. Fortunately, since Myrobalan is still used for hedging, it is possible to get hold of stocks at a very reasonable price. I have planted several, in the hope of having a fruiting hedge of the kind that old fruit growers and orchardists used to grow, but the trees are still very young and I have a few years yet to wait before I shall be able to enjoy the beauty of the flowers and taste for myself those exquisitely shaped, cornelian-coloured little fruits.

Another old plum of great beauty and of exquisite flavour is the Old Transparent gage, the English name for the Reine Claude Diaphane. One cannot read Bunyard's description of this fruit without longing to see and taste it, so marvellously does he call to mind the 'slight flush of red' which first meets the eye, and then one looks 'into the depths of transparent amber as one looks into an opal . . . The flesh is firm . . . and in it are blended all the flavours that a plum can give in generous measure.'

The Reine Claude Diaphane was raised in the early nineteenth century by a Paris nurseryman called Lafay (it was also known as Diaphana Laffay), and brought over to England by Thomas Rivers in about 1845. Rivers had the distinction of raising a fine relative of the Transparent which he called the Early Transparent, from a seedling of the original, which then became known as the Old Transparent. The offspring is self-fertile and a more reliable cropper than its parent, though lacking something in refinement of flavour. It crossed the channel to become a rather unwieldy Early Transparente Reine Claude, or, more gracefully, Reine Claude Diaphane Hative.

The original Reine Claude, and one of the most famous plums of all, is the kind we know as the greengage. It is a plum of great antiquity, believed to have come to Western Europe through Greece from Armenia. It is supposed that since it was named after the wife of Francois I, it reached France during his reign in the late fifteenth or early sixteenth century. This plum, which rapidly gained a reputation as one of the best in Europe, grows fairly true from seed, though minor differences can be detected within the population. With some, the flowers come out before the leaves; with others, it is the other way about; and there are also small distinctions in the colour, leaves and shape of the fruit. In England, in the early sixteenth century, the greengage was called the Verdoch, which suggests that it might come to England by way of Italy, where it was known as Verdoccia. John Parkinson commends the Verdoch plum as 'a fine greene shining plum, fit to preserve'. Greengage jam is still considered to be one of the best-flavoured plum jams. Not so rich in pectin as some of the culinary plums and damsons, it requires less water and keeps its taste well. Its most common English name (there are over two hundred synonyms) is the greengage, which dates from the early eighteenth century when Sir William Gage brought some stocks over from France, and, not knowing the name, called the fruits after himself. George Lindley, a great admirer of the greengage, noted that Sir William procured the stock from the monks of the Chartreuse in Paris. Lindley thought the greengage 'without exception, the best Plum in England with its sweet abundant juice of the richest and most exquisite flavour'. He adds an interesting remark to the effect that the greengage fruit 'when grown upon a healthy standard, and fully exposed to the sun, although not so large, is much richer than when produced against a wall. It is also hardy and an excellent bearer.'

Coe's Golden Drop, another English plum of which George Lindley thought very highly, bears the name of the market gardener who raised it in the late eighteenth century, and is a greengage relative. Jervais Coe told Lindley that his Golden Drop was raised from a stone of a greengage, pollinated, he believed, by the White Magnum Bonum, since the two trees grew almost touching each other in his garden. It was a child of distinguished parents, for the White Magnum Bonum was a plum greatly esteemed in Europe since the early sixteenth century when it was discovered, it is thought, at Besançon. It was originally known in England as the White Imperial and one authority believes it to have been Batty Langley who revised the name: in his *Pomona* (1729) it appears as Mogule Plumb or White Bonum Magnum. This large, yellow plum, which was popular for cooking and preserving, is no longer available (though there is stock at the National Fruit Trials), but its descendent, Coe's Golden Drop, is still to be found in a number of catalogues.

Coe's Golden Drop, Coe's Imperial, or the Bury Seedling (after its place of origin) is a handsome plum, straw coloured, with spots and flecks of rich crimson on its sunny side. Edward Bunyard, with whom it was also a favourite, remarked on its 'pear-like shape and sloping shoulders' and added that 'at its ripest, it is drunk rather than eaten'. Plums usually have to be eaten fairly soon after picking, in fact their quick deterioration is one of the reasons they are not now a popular commercial crop. George Lindley did some experimentation of his own on Coe's Golden Drop, noticing that although 'Ripe the end of September . . . (it) will hang some time upon the tree after it has matured'. He discovered that it would also

> keep for a considerable length of time, after it is gathered, either by suspending it by the stalk upon a string, within side a window facing the sun, or by wrapping it in soft paper and keeping it in a dry room. By this latter method, I have eaten it exceedingly good in October, twelve months after it had been gathered.

Coe's Golden Drop has something of a reputation as a shy cropper, and is ignored by commercial growers, but in private gardens it does well when grown against a sunny wall, and several nurseries sell fan-trained trees for this purpose.

Another choice English plum named after a nurseryman is

Kirke's Plum, also called the Old Brompton because Joseph Kirke's nursery was located in the Brompton Road. Conflicting records of the origin of the seedling which Kirke obtained have never been reconciled. George Lindley, writing in 1831, notes that 'it was brought to notice a few years ago by Mr Kirke of Brompton, and is believed to be of foreign origin'. Everyone seems to be agreed on the excellence of this dark, purplish plum with its remarkably persistent bloom and juicy, well-flavoured greeny-yellow flesh, although they disagree on the quantity of fruit one might expect. Lindley has no hesitation in pronouncing it 'a very handsome variety and an excellent cropper', but Edward Bunyard, while agreeing it to be 'one of the best of black dessert plums', adds that it is 'not a great cropper'. H. V. Taylor in his *Plums of England* reckons it to be 'successful in gardens', though it is not a variety of which commercial growers take any account.

Two putative descendents of Coe's Golden Drop crossed with greengage which should have an honourable mention are the Bryanston and Jefferson plums. The former is an English plum, found at the beginning of the nineteenth century in Lord Portman's gardens at Bryanston Park, Blandford, in Dorset. It is a juicy, yellow dessert plum which matures fairly late for the gage family. The Jefferson, as you might guess from the name, originated in America. A golden-yellow gage of delicious flavour, it was raised by Judge Buel of Albany, New York, in about 1825 and introduced to Britain in 1841. One problem with these in-bred gage plums is that certain varieties will not pollinate others to which they are closely related, so it is necessary to select varieties with great care to ensure full crops. Good catalogues and gardening books give plenty of information about blossoming times, pollen partners and incompatabilities, though for some of the old varieties you may have to consult several sources.

Most of the plums which appeared on the old seventeenth-century lists of Parkinson, Evelyn and Sir Thomas Hanmer have now passed out of all knowledge. The exceptions are damsons, cherry plums, bullaces, and the little yellow plums much liked in France but rare in England, the mirabelles; but perhaps it was not for these that a seventeenth-century scrumper 'climeth over walls, To steal your Plums' as the part song by Dering, written about 1630, has it. Mirabelles are closely allied to damsons and bullaces. The kind known as Mirabelle de Nancy is believed to have come from the east to reach France in the fifteenth century and it is still rated very highly, being placed in Class 1 of the French official list. The Mirabelle de Metz is first recorded in 1675 and is in Class II of the list. Like greengages, these two plums comprise populations of similar individuals rather than clearly defined varieties, and there are often small differences between trees of the same variety. Commercially grown for culinary purposes, conserves and distilling, Mirabelles are nonetheless pleasantly tasty direct from the tree when they are fully ripe.

CHAPTER EIGHT

Cherries Pluck'd Fresh...

Love then unstinted, Love did sip
And Cherries pluck'd fresh from the lip
On Cheeks and Roses free he fed;
Lasses like Autumne Plums did drop
And Lads, indifferently did crop
A Flower, and a Maiden-head
Lovelace: 'Love made in the first Age'

There is a garden in her face
Where roses and white lilies grow;
A heavenly paradise is that place,
Wherein all pleasant fruits do flow,
There Cherries grow which none may buy,
Til 'Cherry-ripe' themselves do cry
Thomas Campion, 1567–1620

Cherry-Ripe, Ripe, Ripe I cry,
Full and faire ones; come and buy:
If so be, you ask me where
They doe grow? I answer, There
Where my Julia's lips doe smile;
There's the Land, or Cherry-Ile;
Whose Plantations fully show
All the yeere, where Cherries grow.
Robert Herrick, 1648

No FRUIT has been so fully identified with the idea of passion and possession as the cherry: so much so that 'cherry lipped' and 'cherry cheeked' were ready-made phrases as far back as the fifteenth century. To seventeenth-century poets the cherry, with its brief perfection, was, like the rose, an emblem both of beauty and mortality, signifying both the pleasures of love and their transience.

Herrick's 'Cherry-ripe' is the best known poem in the genre, but he introduced cherry imagery in a number of other poems, and wrote two wry little verses based on the game of Cherry Chop in which the player trys to bite at a dangling cherry – a game used by him, as by other writers and poets, to signify a sexual teasingness in women:

> Thous gav'st me leave to kiss;
> Thous gav'st me leave to wooe;
> Thous mad'st me thinke by this,
> And that, thou lov'dst me too.

> But I shall ne'er forget,
> How far to make thee merry;
> Thou mad'st me chop, but yet,
> Another snapt the Cherry

The following lyric, written by George Peele in his play *The Old Wives' Tale* (1595), is less innocent than it seems:

> Whenas the rye reach to the chin
> And chopcherry, chopcherry ripe within,
> Strawberrie swimming in the cream,
> And schoolboys playing in the stream;
> Then oh, then oh, my true Love said,
> She could not live a maid.

Shakespeare, too, makes a number of cherry allusions, the two most famous being contained within one scene of *Midsummer Night's Dream* and relating to Helena and Hermia. Demetrius, after a period of aberration following a dose of Puck's love-drops, wakes restored and full of hyperbole in favour of his true love, Helena:

> ... goddess, nymph, perfect, divine!
> To what my love shall I compare thine eyne?
> Crystal is muddy. O! how ripe in show
> Thy lips, those kissing Cherries, tempting grow ...

and much else. Helena herself seeks a less commonplace image to describe her close friendship with Hermia.

So we grew together,
Like to a double cherry, seeming parted,
But yet an union in partition;
Two lovely berries moulded on one stem;
So with two seeming bodies, but one heart;

Double cherries are rarities, like four-leaved clovers. I have only found them twice and they must have been equally unusual in Shakespeare's day, for the comparison is with a very special relationship. Later in this scene Shakespeare returns indirectly to this cherry simile, when Hermia turns against Helena's apparent treachery and begins a burst of invective with the words 'thou canker blossom'. As a matter of fact, cherries are often spoiled by attacks of bacterial canker, to which they are particularly vulnerable.

In art as in poetry, the cherry symbolized the sweetness of earthly life. In religious painting, the cherry and the apple (or pear) are often placed in opposition, standing for the joys and sorrows of the life of Christ. In Memling's picture in the Uffizi, the Christ child holds cherries in one hand, while with the other He takes an apple from an angel. In the *Madonna and Child* of Carlo Crivelli and of Giorgio Schiavone (both in The National Gallery, London) and in many other Renaissance pictures, the same theme occurs with minor variations. The cherry is also prominent among the fruit trees which are set against the apple, or the Tree of Knowledge of Good and Evil, in Robert Laneham's account (1575) of the lovely garden at Kenilworth. He plays on the idea of the Paradise garden and dwells almost languishingly on its sensual delights, only drawing back just in time to attribute the plenitude to God and to add a moral postscript.

A garden then so appointed, as wherein aloft upon sweet shadowed walk of terrace; in heat of summer to feel the pleasant whisking wind above, or delectable coolness of the fountain-spring beneath, to taste of delicious strawberries, cherries and other fruits, even from their stalks; to smell such fragrancy of sweet odours, breathing from the plants, herbs and flowers; to hear such natural melodious music and tunes of birds; to have in eye for mirth sometime these underspringing streams; then the woods, the waters (for both pool and chase were hard at hand in sight), the deer, the people . . . the fruit trees, the plants, the herbs, the flowers, the change in colours, the birds flittering, the fountain streaming, the fish swimming, all in such delectable variety, order and dignity; whereby at one moment, in one place, at hand, without travel, to have so full fruition of so many God's blessings, by entire delight unto all senses (if all can take) at once; for etymon of the word worthy to be called Paradise; and though not so goodly as Paradise for want of the fair rivers, yet a great deal by the lack of so unhappy a tree.

Strawberries and cherries are mentioned together in an early Household Book (Althorpe MS) where there is an entry for 1636 for 'Weedeing & setting strawberries in the cherry yarde'. This gardening practice extends into the present day, for I have come across several modern horticulturists who recommend the growing of soft fruits such as strawberries or blackcurrants in the cherry orchard. Cherries come slowly to bearing fruit and reaching their full span, and the ground can be profitably utilized now as in the past with a soft fruit crop. The phrase 'cherry yarde' in the Althorpe MS is also to be found in fifteenth-century accounts of Norwich Priory, which also mention an 'appleyarde' and even a 'grasyarde'.

There are many other clues beside these early 'cherry yeardes' indicating that cherries were a passion for the English from at least the beginning of the Middle Ages. People of all classes seem to have enjoyed them: 'Many a one is fond of them,' noted Chaucer in *The Romaunt of the Rose*, and in Langland's *Piers Plowman* it was the poor people who brought Piers Plowman 'chibolles & chervelys and ripe chiries monye' to assuage his hunger.

At the other end of the social scale, Francis Bacon recommends that cherry trees should be planted in a prince's garden, and so they were. When Queen Henrietta Maria's garden at Wimbledon was catalogued by the parliamentary surveyors, their report listed a hundred and fifty-seven cherry trees. Some were in the kitchen garden but most, which were 'well planted and ordered, and of a great growth in themselves', were to be found in the upper garden where there were also a number of wall-trained fruit trees which included cherries. Fruit trees, but cherries in particular, were appreciated for their beauty as well as for their fruit. The great garden at Deepdene, as shown in a sketch by John Aubrey, has an orchard entirely devoted to cherries, which did not prevent their also being planted along the walks; and at the Earl of Pembroke's showpiece at Wilton there was a large garden, with the Borghese gladiator as centrepiece, laid out to formal walks, and lined exclusively with cherry trees. In the chapter on 'Ornaments' in his *A New Orchard and Garden*, William Lawson suggests that 'mounts' should be covered with fruit

Jargonelle

Glou Morceau

Frogmore Early

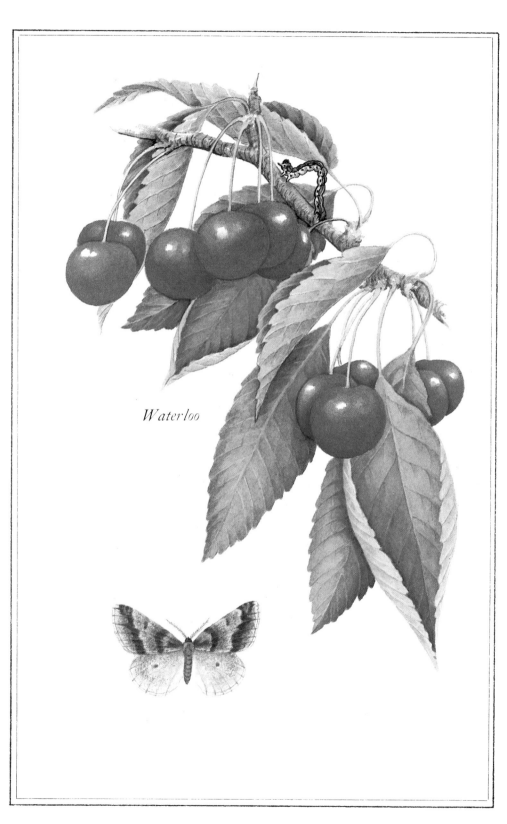

Waterloo

trees such as Kentish cherries, damsons and plums, as well as with man-made decorations.

In the early thirteenth century Alexander Neckham included cherries among the 'noble fruit', along with medlars and plums (*'mespila cum cerasis et prunis'*) in his poem *De Laudibus Divinae Sapientiae*. In his *De Naturis Rerum* he mentions cherries again, noting that they and certain other fruits should be eaten on a fasting stomach, a notion which like much else in these two works he picked up from classical authors. John Russell in his *Boke of Nurture* similarly instructs his readers to 'eat cherries fasting', but a later writer, John Parkinson, says quite firmly that all of the thirty-five varieties of cherry that he describes 'serve wholly to please the palate and are eaten at all times, both before and after meals'.

Henry VIII had a well-known preference for cherries, and his fruiterer, Richard Harris, planted the 'New Garden' at Teynham in Kent with many fine cherry trees brought from Holland. This was the beginning of a campaign to produce enough home-grown fruit of excellence to compete with the fruit which was being imported to Billingsgate from France and the Low Countries. According to a pamphlet of 1604, *The Husbandman's Fruitful Orchard*, these trees prospered and supplied many grafts to other English orchards.

We can surmise that Henry VIII's liking for cherries was passed on to Queen Elizabeth from a graceful story recorded by Sir Hugh Plat concerning 'a conceit of that delicate knight' Sir Francis Carew, when the Queen visited him at Beddington. He covered a cherry tree with canvas kept damp to retard the fruit, only removing the tent when assured of Her Majesty's coming, 'so that she had cherries at least one moneth after all cherries had taken their farewell of England.'

It was not unusual for fruit to be presented as a token of affection or esteem. Nowadays, as a rule, we make gifts of fruit only to people who are ill, but in Tudor times it was an acceptable gift in any circumstances. The Duke of Buckingham's household accounts show that he was pleased to receive a dish of cherries sent by the Bishop of Norwich. Diana's maid in Spenser's *Faerie Queene* was allured not only with 'flattering words' but also with '. . . pleasing gifts for her purvey'd / Queen-apples and red cherries from the tree.'

The cherry orchards of Norfolk and Kent were specially remarked upon by William Bulleyn in his *Newe Book entitled the Government of Healthe* (1558). There were Huguenot settlements in both regions, and the immigrants brought with them their skill in fruit growing. Richard Harris, setting up the King's 'New Garden' at Teynham, had 'fetched out of the Lowe Countries, cherrie grafts...' However, *The Husbandman's Fruitful Orchard* notes that 'there was some store of fruite in England', and there are certainly references to thriving cherry orchards well before the Huguenots began to make their impact. A Pipe Roll from Suffolk accounts the money brought in from 'apples, and cherries' sold by a certain manor in the Honour of Clare in 1236. Fitzherbert, in his treatise on husbandry (published in 1523 with many subsequent editions), reckoned cherries among the profitable fruits for a husbandman to grow.

There were almost certainly orchards in Kent before the Teynham development. It was in many ways an ideal spot for cherry growing. Not only were the soil and climate suitable, but the ripe and easily perishable fruit could reach London by river (the Stour or the Medway and Thames) quickly enough to be sold while still at its peak.

The anonymous *London Licpenye* (previously ascribed to Lydgate) is a witty, ironic poem about how a 'man of Kent' comes up to London to seek justice for a grievance and finds again and again, not only in Westminster but also in the streets and the busy markets, that 'they that lacked money, myght not spede', until finally he decides to cut his losses and return home. Between Westminster gate and Cheapside he is offered fruit and flowers by street sellers, among which goods are 'Strabery rype, and chery in the ryse'. Practically every book which quotes this line has a note to the effect that 'in the ryse' means 'on the branch', or sometimes more particularly 'on the spur': that is, the spur or shoot cut off with the cherries still attached. This is puzzling, because cherries fruit most vigorously on one- or two-year-old wood. They are never 'spur-pruned' as apples are, because to remove spurs and shoots would be to remove that best fruit-bearing wood; and I am sure that early fruit gardeners were sufficiently skilled in their trade to know this. In fact, *The Husbandman's Fruitful Orchard* is quite clear in its instruction to break no stalk except that by which the cherry hangs.

I have not seen any early explanation of the meaning of 'in the ryse', but in the Mauron-Tempest *Cryes of the City of London* (1688) there is an illustration of a lady with a basket of cherries which appear to have leaves and twigs. Who is to say whether this is authentic? There are many other engravings which show cherries in baskets or barrows with only their stalks attached. In several of these, there are shown small sticks with cherries tied to them in ones or twos, the sticks themselves, in some cases, stuck upright into the wicker baskets. I have no evidence that cherries sold on sticks in this way were known as 'cherries in the ryse' but it does seem to be at least a possibility.

The 'Cherry Ripe' cry lifted by Herrick for his famous lyric is by no means the only cherry cry. There was 'Round and Sound / Twopence a pound / Cherries, rare ripe cherries,' quoted in *Hone's Every-day Book*, and there were even a few cries which specified the variety: 'Round and sound, fivepence a pound, Duke Cherries . . .' and 'Black and white heart cherries' and 'fine bigaroon cherries' (collected in *The London Spy*, 1703).

Cherry trees like a loamy, well-drained soil and do well when this lies over chalk, though this is not essential. Kent is the most famed cherry-growing region but there are other areas where cherry orchards prosper, principally in Hertfordshire, Buckinghamshire, Herefordshire and Worcestershire. The Hertfordshire orchards are the most recently developed, having received a considerable boost when the railway to London was opened giving a new means by which perfectly ripe fruit could get quickly to the markets. There are many regional varieties of cherry, and out of about fifty local named varieties I have come across, all except one or two are attributed to one or another of these three areas. A great many Hart or Heart cherry varieties come from Hertfordshire, but I think this was a latterday punning adoption because the name originally seems to have derived from shape rather than place, and there are many other regions which grow Hearts. Parkinson (1629) described the Lesser and Greater Hart cherries (also called Lacures): 'full above, and a little pointing downward, after the fashion of an heart, as it is usually painted. . . .'

Among the local varieties recorded from Hertfordshire and Buckinghamshire by Grubb in 1949 were Alba Heart, August Heart, Ronald's Heart, Smoky Heart and Strawberry Heart. Though few cherries are now grown in parts of Hertfordshire such as King's Langley, once famous for its cherry orchards, the roads of some villages retain old names such as Cherry Bounce and there are still big, old cherry trees to be seen by the wayside.

Grubb, a man not given to excitement, allows himself a touch of enthusiasm when he recalls the largest cherry trees he ever saw.

These were Corones, called Croomes in Watford where he saw them. Corones, caroons, croomes or croons are a very old and popular kind of cherry. They came only moderately true from seed, which accounts for the different characteristics of trees grown in different localities. Hogg (1862) gives Black Bud of Buckinghamshire as an alternative name for Corone; it was possibly one of this kind which Grubb saw a century later in neighbouring Hertfordshire. 'The Corone Cherrie' was among the varieties which Parkinson records, though his tree differs in its particulars from more modern descriptions.

The local events known as Cherry Fairs were markets combined with festivity. Halliwell mentions that the Cherry Fairs of Worcestershire were still held a hundred years ago and in Hertfordshire there were still fairs in the early twentieth century. Cherry fairs found their way into literature as a metaphor of the short sweetness of life and its earthly pleasures. In *Confessio Amantis* (1393), John Gower, a contemporary and friend of Chaucer, wrote of both cherry feasts and cherry fairs: 'For al is but a chery feire. This worldes good'. A little later Thomas Hoccleve uses the same image in *The regement of Princes*: 'Thy life my sone is but a chery feire'. There is a glancing reference in *Piers Plowman* which links the brevity of earthly pleasures and the lastingness of sin simply by identifying a moment of transgression with this festival time. 'Peronella, a priest's child, would never be prioress, / For she had a child at cherry-time, as all the chapter knew.'

Harvesting cherries is a tricky and labour-intensive business. Cherry trees tend to be large and only very recently has it become possible to graft them on to less vigorous stock, so picking cherries traditionally entails considerable use of ladders. The fruit must be picked ripe, and since all the cherries on a tree do not ripen at the same time the trees have to be picked over several times during the short season. These considerations, rather than a shift in public taste, mainly explain why there are fewer cherries about nowadays. Also, neither supermarkets nor greengrocers like short-lived, delicate fruit, however delicious.

Fruit garden enthusiasts do not, however, have marketing constraints. A private gardener can pick and use his or her fruit as it ripens, and take pleasure in the labour. *The Husbandman's Fruitful Orchard* describes the method (most of this is still sound advice):

They are not ripe all at once, nor may be gathered at once, therefore with a light Ladder, made to stand of itself without hurting the boughs, mount to the Tree, and with a gathering-hook, gather those which be full ripe, and put them into your Cherry-pot, or Kybzey hanging by your side, or upon any bough you please, and be sure to break no stalk, but that the cherry hangs by, and pull them gently, lay them down tenderly, and handle them as little as you can.

For the conveyance or portage of Cherries, they are best to be carried in broad Baskets, like sives, with smooth yielding bottoms, only two broad laths going along the bottom; and be filled in the top, lest setting one upon another, you bruise and hurt the Cherries; if you carry by horse-back, then panniers well lined with Fern, and packt full and close, is the best and safest way.

Many of the old recipes for cherries involve drying, pickling or making cheeses or pastes as a means of keeping them beyond their short season, but they were also enjoyed fresh or in pies and tarts. As Gerard remarks in passing, 'Many excellent Tarts and other pleasant meets are made with Cherries, sugar and other delicate spices'. There was even a particular variety known as 'Pie Cherry', otherwise The Kentish Red. Some recipes specify varieties, in particular Kentish cherries. While much of the country was glad to have cherries in any form, regions such as Kent, where they were plentiful, developed local specialities designed to stimulate tired palates since appreciation, even of the best fruit, wanes when there is a great deal of it. Cherry Batter, which comes from Tunbridge Wells, is a special batter which is lightly fried and served on a pile of hot baked cherries. Cherry Huffkins are a Kentish tea-bread with a hole in the centre, filled with hot cherries.

Milton, said Samuel Johnson, 'could cut a Colossus from a rock; but . . . not carve heads upon cherry-stones'. The idea of this miniature skill seems more familiar than could be explained by that single reference to it, yet I have been unable to trace any other and have never seen a carved cherry stone. I have, however, seen them employed in a game known by Shakespeare as Cherry-pit. In *Twelfth Night* Malvolio is taunted by Sir Toby Belch who says 'What man, 'tis not for gravity to play at cherrie-pit with Satan.' The game can also be called Cherry-stone (an early sixteenth-century text declares 'Playenge at cheriston is good for Children') and is usually described as the throwing of cherry stones into a small pit or hole. The version I learnt was rather ruder: we spat our stones at the target. We also used to make ear-rings out of two cherries on a joined stalk, but we had no special name for this game. I have since seen it referred to as Cherry-bob.

Like a number of other well-liked fruits, the cherry was the subject of a riddle-rhyme:

> *Riddle me riddle me ree*
> *A little man in a tree*
> *A staff in his hand,*
> *A stone in his throat,*
> *If you read me this riddle*
> *I'll give you a groat.*

Another old jingle, obviously made more for the rhyme's sake than as a prophecy, is 'A cherry year, a merry year'; and 'cherry merry' was sometimes said of a person in his or her cups.

Cherry brandy was also known as Cherry Bounce, though this could also refer to brandy with sugar added. Not surprisingly, the main manufacturer of cherry brandy operates in Kent. The firm of Grants of Maidstone supplied Queen Victoria with this liqueur, which she is said to have greatly enjoyed. Most recipes for it specify Morello cherries, but Eliza Acton says it can also be made from 'small cherries called in the markets Brandy blacks' – presumably another sour cherry. The method is simple: fill a wide-necked bottle two-thirds full of cherries, add four ounces of brown or white candy sugar and fill it up with good brandy to reach the neck of the bottle. Cork, and stand it for two months. This makes splendid brandied cherries as well as an excellent liqueur, and is a good way to use sharp cherries if you have such a tree in your garden.

Until recently a garden had to be fairly extensive before cherries could be considered, because a healthy standard tree in fertile soil will reach a spread of about forty feet. It was only during the 1970s that attempts to graft cherries on to a rather more dwarfing rootstock at last succeeded; now they can be bought on 'Colt', which gives a less vigorous growth. Bushes and fan-trained trees can be planted fifteen feet apart, while pyramids can have as little as twelve feet between them. When there is space only for a single cherry tree, a Morello is the usual choice because it is one of the few cherries which is completely self-compatible and can therefore pollinate itself. There is only one self-fertile sweet cherry. A modern variety, with the name Stella; it originated in Summerland, British Columbia and was introduced to Britain in 1968.

Morello cherries can be eaten raw when fully ripe, but are famous for their use in cooking, wine and brandy. The name is probably derived from the Italian word *amarella*, meaning bitter, but there are several varieties or forms of Morello, and some are less harsh than others. Wye Morello is a clone used principally in the making of cherry brandy. In the past Morello cherries, also called Late-ripe cherries, were often kept for winter use.

> The late ripe Cherries which the French-men keep dried against winter, and are by them called *Morelle*, and we after the same name call them Morell Cherries, are dry, and do somewhat binde, these being dried are pleasant to the taste, and wholesome to the stomacke ...

wrote Gerard in 1597; and Parkinson too thought well of Morellos which he describes as:

> of a darke red colour when they are full ripe, and hang long on, of a sweetish sower taste, the pulpe or substance is red, and somewhat firme: if they be dryed they will have a fine sharpe or sower taste very delectable.

The famous Kentish Red, mentioned by Evelyn, is a type known as *Amarelle*. Also a culinary cherry, it has red fruits and transparent juice, as opposed to the Morello's crimson-black skin and red juice. Both these types of cherry are thought to have derived from the dwarf cherry, *Prunus Cerasus*, which is commonly naturalized in Britain as a wild population, quite probably descending from the Morellos and Amarelles of early orchards and fruit gardens. The Kentish Red tree, like the Morello, is rather smaller than a sweet cherry; it is also self-compatible, and is suitable for smaller gardens – if it can be found. It is a great deal more difficult to trace than the Morello, but it has long been commended for its juicy scarlet fruits, which are among the best for bottling and jam making. (Eliza Acton has two jam recipes which specify that these or the similar Flemish cherry should be used.) The Kentish Red tree also has a good resistance to bacterial canker.

Most of the modern sweet cherries available in nurseries had their beginnings in the work of Thomas Andrew Knight in the early nineteenth century. An early president of the Royal Horticultural Society, and author of the classic *Pomona Herefordiensis* (1811), he concentrated considerable effort into the hybridization and cross-pollination of cherries. He is commemorated by name in the variety

Knight's Early Black, and he raised other equally famous fore-runners such as Elton Heart and Waterloo. Waterloo, introduced in 1815, is still recommended for flavour, and is available from several nurseries.

The most important ancestor of the sweet cherry is the native wild cherry, *Prunus Avium*, which is often pleasantly sweet. Out of fashion now is an ancient group of cherries known as Duke cherries (as in the old street cries). The origins of these are obscure but they are believed to have resulted from hybridization between the sour cherry and the sweet. They are very difficult to find today. I have managed to find only Archduke, which is on Parkinson's list, and May Duke, another old variety. Both are highly praised for flavour by Bunyard. Another old variety still available from one nursery is Belle de Chatenay, a crimson cherry, yellow inside, juicy and slightly bittersweet. However, as it has only moderate fertility, it is, as Bunyard notes, 'a fruit to be grown only by those who put quality first'.

The Merton cherries raised at the John Innes Institute since the Second World War are among the most widely sold and recom-mended sweet cherries in most present-day catalogues, but some-times there are still some nineteenth-century varieties in the lists. Besides Waterloo, there are Frogmore Early, raised by Mr Thomas Ingram of Frogmore Gardens, Hampstead in about 1864 (a good tree for garden or orchard); and Early Rivers, described by one nurseryman as 'the prince of cherries'. Raised by Thomas Rivers of the famous Hertfordshire nursery and introduced about 1872, this cherry has a delicious flavour and can usually be relied upon for a good crop of dark 'melting and deliciously flavoured' fruit.

Unfortunately, it is not always possible to have the cherries you most want to grow, since they are so choosy in their pollen partners. It is important to consult a reliable authority when making your selection. I would advise anyone to doublecheck all information and to talk to a good nurseryman as well, since a mistake takes a long time to show up, and, if you have to plant an extra pollinator, even longer to put right.

Some ancient cherry varieties have disappeared entirely: the Gascoigns, for example, so highly esteemed by John Parkinson as stocks for the May cherry, though it was hard to come by true Gascoigns even in his time. They were, it appears, a kind of wild cherry which used to be imported from Gascony. Their name lingers on in 'gaskins', used in the south of England for the gean or wild cherry, *Prunus avium*. (Gean itself is the English version of the French *guigne*, the word for heart cherry.) Another vernacular name for the wild cherry is mazzard, which I think may derive, like so many cherry names, from the French, in this case from *merise*, a wild cherry. Alternative forms of mazzard were mazar and maser. The wild cherry is a large, graceful tree to be found in woodlands all over Britain, and is to my mind the most beautiful of all the cherries. Though I see it springtime after springtime, I am never quite prepared for the beauty of the woodland cherry covered in white blossom, somehow more striking within the thick growth of a forest than it would be in an artificial setting.

Afterword

THE EARLIEST picture of an orchard that I know of occurs in an illuminated fourteenth-century manuscript, a translation of Bartholemew the Englishman's *De Proprietatibus Rerum*. It shows a small orchard enclosed by a wattle fence, inside which a figure, apparently a woman, is reaching up for an apple with an expression of extreme delight and anticipation on her face. I have looked at several hundred pictures of gardens and orchards, from the earliest fenced enclosures, the medieval trellised gardens and the walled *hortus conclusus*, to the magnificent concerns of Wilton Palace and other noble estates; and always, where people are represented, it is with such an expression of pride and pleasure.

The medieval gatherings depicted in the garden of *Le Roman de la Rose* in the famous edition painted about 1475, show the participants sitting under the fruit trees, singing and dancing beside the fountains and dallying in the walks. In a less idealistic setting of the same period, the orchard owner illustrated in *Le Livre de Rustican* is giving instructions about the harvesting which is going on behind him. The scene is one of fruitfulness and activity: you can see the main orchard, espaliered fruits on the house, and small trees in enclosed gardens. People in trees and up ladders are gathering in the apples. In the distance a pig has upset one of the heaped baskets and is greedily helping itself to the contents. A fruit garden, rather than an orchard, is the frontispiece for *The Gentleman's Recreation* by John Lawrence (1716) which shows a formal but not very large garden, in which two gentlemen are carrying on a discussion (possibly about the fruits around them), a dog plays, and a woman and child are walking down one of the paths. The four rectangular plots are planted with dwarf fruit trees and the walls of the garden are covered with espaliered trees. Isaac de Caus' design for Wilton is formality on an infinitely grander scale, but even here people, though diminutive in size, are shown wandering round the gardens, enjoying the cherry tree walks and the arbours of the gladiator garden.

The old gardening writers saw fruit gardening as a labour of love, and the orchard as a place where the work of gardening refreshes, rather than tires. William Lawson goes so far as to say:

> The principal end of an Orchard, is the honest delight of one wearied with the work of his lawful calling. . . . The very works of, and in an Orchard and Garden, are better than the ease and rest of, and from other labours.

And for important men of affairs, the orchard is even more a necessity:

> . . . whither do they withdraw themselves from the troublesome affairs of their estate, being tired with the hearing and judging of litigious Controversies, choaken (as it were) with the close air of their sumptuous Buildings, their stomachs cloyed with variety of Banquets, their ears filled and over-burthened with tedious discoursings? Whither but into their Orchards, made and prepared, dressed and destinated for that purpose, to renew and refresh their senses, and to call home their over-wearied spirits? Nay it is (no doubt) a comfort to them, to set open their casements into a most delicate Garden and Orchard, whereby they may not only see that, wherein they so much delighted, but also to give fresh sweet and pleasant air to their Galleries and Chambers.

And the pleasures of such great men, can, he concludes, be ours too if we open our eyes to the joys of work in an orchard.

The associations carried by orchards and fruits, are all of a positive tenor. Indeed the word fruitful has become almost synonymous with lifegiving in a general context. Many writers have seen in the idea of an orchard an emblem of God's work. For Leonard Mascall, 'Nothing more discovereth unto us the great incomprehensible worke of God, that of one little Pepin sede . . . may come to the selfsame herb or tree and to bring forth infinite of the same fruit, which also doth shine and shew forth its selfe unto us.'

Fruit gardening in the seventeenth and eighteenth centuries was regarded as an intellectually satisfying pursuit in a way which is ignored nowadays. Alongside Lawson's orchardists of 'greatness and ability' Meager enlists others of 'generous and active mind', setting out the sum of the pleasure that fruit trees give, in relation to the expense of planting up an orchard.

> As for the Charge of raising and planting Fruit-trees, considering the Years they must stand and the continual Encrease, I look upon it as trivial, considering the Recompense they will soon make, besides the Abundance of

Pleasure it must be to any generous and active Mind to see flourishing Trees of his own setting, and peaceably enjoy himself in Contemplation, under the cooling Shades of their spreading Branches . . .

In a sense, the planting of fruit trees is a pledge of faith in the future, and even, perhaps especially, when the future is uncertain, it is important to make the gesture. Nowhere is this more clearly expressed than by the peasant farmer Marcel Nicoud, as recounted by John Berger in *Pig Earth*, his remarkable narrative about peasant culture in the south of France. 'Marcel was the only man in the village who planted new apple trees . . . The other men reasoned that the old trees – some of them were perhaps two hundred years old – would last their lifetime and that afterwards the orchards would be abandoned . . .'
This is how he explained planting the new apple trees.

My sons won't work on the farm. They want to have free week-ends and fixed hours. They like to have money in their pockets so as to be able to spend it. They have gone to earn money and are mad about it. Michel has gone to work in a factory. Edouard has gone into commerce. (He used the term commerce because he did not wish to be harsh towards his younger son.) I believe they are mistaken. Selling things all day, or working forty-five hours a week in a factory is no life for a man – jobs like that will lead to ignorance. It is unlikely that they will ever work this farm. The farm will end with Nicole and me. Why work with such effort and care for something which is doomed? And to that I reply: Working is a way of preserving the knowledge my sons are losing. I dig the holes, wait for the tender moon and plant out these saplings to give an example to my sons if they are interested, and, if not, to show my father and his father that the knowledge they handed down has not yet been abandoned. Without that knowledge I am nothing.

We are far from a peasant way of life but the general point holds true in its widest sense. The knowledge of our forebears is culturally important to us, and we honour them in conserving the fruit of their labour; in justly cherishing the varieties they sought and bred and tended with such care, we enrich both our lives and the lives of generations to come.
For the last word I turn again to William Lawson, surely the greatest advocate of the orchard and fruit garden.

Now pause with your self, and view the end of all your Labours in an Orchard: unspeakable pleasure and infinite commodity.

APPENDIX I

Nurseries

The following is a selection of nurseries which have a good range of fruits and which produce catalogues. (It is worth noting that I talked to almost as many again who held comparatively good stocks but did not have catalogues, so it is worth checking on local nurseries to find out what they have, before going further afield.) Catalogues are expensive to produce, so most nurseries make a small charge for them, but since they often contain planting and gardening notes, they are usually worth the outlay. It is wise to place your orders early, especially for some of the rarer items – and always check that the varieties you are after are available, as stocks vary from year to year and during a season. If the variety you are seeking is not listed, it is well worth the effort of telephoning a few nurseries; many of them hold a wider range than their catalogues say. If this fails, write to the Fruit Officer, Royal Horticultural Society's Garden, Wisley, Woking, Surrey.

The number of varieties of each fruit stocked is given in brackets.

J. C. Allgrove Ltd, The Nursery, Middle Green, Langley, Buckinghamshire.
  Tel: Slough (0753) 20155
A very good selection, especially of apples, with some rare varieties and a huge choice. Many varieties not listed are also available on application including a Bullace plum called the Langley Bullace. Apples (155); Pears (24); Plums (28); Cherries (18); Peaches (13); Nectarines (7); Apricots (4); Quince (3); Medlar; Cob nut; Red currants (4); White currants (3); Black currants (7); Raspberries (12); Strawberries (2); Blackberries (3); Gooseberries (16); Loganberry; Figs (2); Grape vines (3).

Aylett's Nurseries Ltd, North Orbital Road, St Albans, Hertfordshire AL2 1DH.
  Tel: Bowmansgreen (0727) 22255
A large and varied stock of fruit; useful list with hints on planting and care; advice on planning fruit garden offered. Apples (29); Pears (11); Plums (11); Cherries (11); Peaches (5); Nectarines (2); Apricot; Quince; Medlar; Mulberry; Crab apples (4); Walnut; Chestnut; Cob nut; Sweet almond; Red currants (3); White currants (2); Black currants (9); Raspberries (12); Straw-

berries (3); Blackberries (4); Gooseberries (4); Loganberries (2); Blueberries (2); Figs (2); Grape vines (11).

Bayley's Garden Centre and Nurseries, Bayston Hill, near Shrewsbury, Shropshire SY3 0DA. *Tel:* Bayston Hill (074372) 4261/2
Apples (20); Pears (5); Plums (11); Cherry; Peach; Nectarine; Apricot; Red currant; White currant; Black currant; Raspberries (7); Strawberries (3); Blackberries (2); Gooseberries (3); Loganberries (2).

C. A. Boniface & Sons Ltd, Garden Centre and Nurseries, 15 Sandy Brow, Purbrook, Portsmouth, Hampshire PO7 5JP. *Tel:* Waterlooville (07014) 3454
No fruit catalogue issued, phone for details. Apples (30); Pears (4); Plums (8); Cherries (3); Peaches (4); Nectarines (2); Apricot; Red currant; Black currants (3); Raspberries (2); Blackberry; Loganberry; Gooseberry.

Bridgemere Nurseries Ltd, Bridgemere, near Nantwich, Cheshire. *Tel:* Bridgemere (09365) 239
Apples (32); Pears (8); Plums (5); Cherries (5); Peaches (2); Quince; Walnut; Crab apples (2); Raspberries (6); Strawberries (4); Blackberries (3); Gooseberries (4); Loganberry; Fig; Grape vines (6).

Cheals Garden Centre, Horsham Road, Crawley, West Sussex. *Tel:* Crawley (0293) 22101
Several apples stocked that are not in the list; also family trees triple and double grafted (though with standard Delicious/Cox combinations). Apples (23); Pears (4); Plums (4); Cherries (2); Peaches (3); Nectarine; Quince (2); Mulberries (2); Red currant; White currant; Black currants (3); Raspberries (4); Strawberries (2); Blackberries (3); Gooseberries (3); Loganberries (3); Blueberry; Fig; Grape vine (4).

W. Crowder and Sons Ltd, Thimbleby Nurseries, Horncastle, Lincolnshire. *Tel:* Horncastle (06582) 6363
Apples (17); Pears (7); Plums (11); Cherries (5); Peach; Apricot; Walnut; Red currant; White currant; Black currants (2); Raspberries (2); Strawberries (2); Blackberry; Gooseberries (5); Loganberry; Grape vine.

Deacons Nursery, Moor View House, Godshill, Isle of Wight PO38 3HW. *Tel:* Godshill (098389) 750 & 778
A wide range of fruit with an exceptional number of 'family trees' including a 'fruit and nut' tree! Five kinds of hazel. Also good crab apples and some cider apples. Apples (92); Pears (11); Plums (20); Cherries (14); Peaches (10); Nectarines (3); Apricots (6); Quince (2); Crab apples (5); Medlar (3); Mulberry (2); Cob nuts (5); Walnut (2); Red currants (6); White currants (2);

Black currants (9); Raspberries (7); Strawberries (7); Blackberries (7); Gooseberries (9); Loganberries (2); Fig; Grape vines (5).

Everton Nurseries Ltd, Everton, near Lymington, Hampshire, so4 ojz. *Tel:* Milford-on-Sea (059069) 2155
Apples (26); Pears (8); Plums (14); Cherries (8); Peaches (3); Nectarines (3); Apricot; Quince; Mulberry; Crab apples (5); Chestnut; Cobnut; Red currant; White currant; Black currants (2); Gooseberries (3); Raspberries (6); Straw-berries (5); Blackberry; Loganberries (2); Fig; Grape vines (8).

Fairfield Nurseries (Hermitage) Ltd, Hermitage, Newbury, Berkshire, RG16 9TG. *Tel:* Hermitage (0635) 200442
Large nursery and garden centre, with fruit and vegetable shop attached, selling own produce in season. May stock plants not in catalogue. Good raspberry selection. Apples (20); Pears (5); Plums (8); Cherries (7); Peaches (3); Nectarine; Apricot; Quince (2); Cob nut; Medlar; Red currant; White currant; Black currants (5); Raspberries (8); Strawberries (4); Blackberries (2); Gooseberries (5); Loganberry; Fig; Grape vines (11).

A. Goatcher and Son, The Nurseries, Washington, near Pulborough, Sussex. *Tel:* Ashington (0903) 892626
A large nursery of over forty acres with experience of 130 years or so behind them. Advice given (enclose s.a.e. if postal enquiry). Apples (23); Pears (5); Plums (10); Cherries (5); Peaches (5); Nectarines (3); Apricot; Quince; Medlar; Mulberry; Walnut; Red currant; Black currants (3); Raspberries (3); Blackberries (3); Gooseberries (2); Loganberries (2); Fig.

W. H. Harris, Westacott Nursery, Barnstaple, Devon. *Tel:* Barnstaple (0271) 3762
Excellent selection of cider apples. Two kinds of filbert. Advice given. Apples (63); Pears (9); Plums (7); Cherries (4); Peaches (3); Nectarines; Apricot; Quince; Mulberry; Crab apples (2); Cob nut (2); Sweet chestnut; Red currant; White currant; Black currants (5); Raspberries (7); Strawberries (4); Blackberries (2); Gooseberries (6); Loganberries (2); Fig; Grape vines (2+).

Highfield Nurseries, Whitminster, Gloucester. *Tel:* Gloucester (0452) 740266
Advice given – telephone or postal (send s.a.e.). Good catalogue, personal service. Apples (26); Pears (5); Plums (7); Cherries (4); Peaches (3); Nec-tarine; Apricot; Quince; Medlar; Walnut; Cob nut; Red currant; White currant; Black currants (3); Raspberries (6); Strawberries (6); Blackberries (4); Loganberry; Blueberries (2); Fig; Grape vines (7).

R. Hill and Son, Nurserymen, Appleton, Abingdon, Oxfordshire OX13 5QN.
    Tel: Cumnor (08676) 2081
Soft fruits only, but they stock standard gooseberries in several varieties, and
Myrobalan plums. Red currants (2); White currant; Black currants (10); Rasp-
berries (2); Gooseberries (12); Myrobalan plum.

Hillier Nurseries (Winchester) Ltd, Ampfield House, Ampfield, Romsey,
    Hampshire SO5 9PA. *Tel:* Braishfield (0794) 68733
Unusual in stocking wild service, *Sorbus domestica* and cranberry (*Vaccinium
macrocarpum*). Also named varieties of walnut and both black and white
mulberry. Apples (22); Pears (5); Plums (10); Cherries (4); Peaches (2);
Nectarine; Apricot; Quince; Mulberries (3); Medlar; Crab apple; Walnut;
Cob nut; Red currants (2); White currant; Black currants (2); Raspberries
(2); Strawberries (5); Blackberry; Gooseberries (3); Loganberry; Blueberry;
Cranberry; Fig; Grape vines (5); Wild Service and *Sorbus domestica*.

Jackmans Nurseries Ltd, Woking, Surrey. *Tel:* Woking (04862) 4861
Several varieties of cob nut/filbert available; also alpine strawberries and good
selection of grape vines. Apples (14); Pears (4); Plums (6); Cherries (3);
Peaches (2); Nectarine; Mulberry; Apricot; Cob nut; Walnut; Red currant;
White currant; Black currants (3); Gooseberries (4); Loganberries (2); Rasp-
berries (7); Strawberries (8); Blackberries (2); Fig; Grape vines (20).

John Jefferies and Son Ltd, Cirencester, Gloucestershire GL7 1QB. *Tel:*
    Cirencester (0285) 2202
One of the few who stock Dutch quince. Apples (21); Pears (4); Plum;
Peaches (4); Quince; Crab apples (4); Medlar; Red currants (2); Black cur-
rants (3); Raspberries (4); Strawberries (3); Blackberry; Gooseberries (3);
Loganberry; Grape vine.

Keepers Nursery, 446 Wateringbury Road, East Malling, Maidstone, Kent.
    Tel: Maidstone (0622) 813008
One of the few to sell Wilson's Long Bunch red currants, the only surviving
late old variety. Apples (56); Pears (18); Plums (19;) Cherries (17); Peach;
Walnut; Cob nut; Red currants (3); White currant; Black currants (9);
Raspberries (8); Strawberries (3); Gooseberries (5).

New Tree Nurseries (P. H. Harding), 2 Nunnery Road, Canterbury, Kent
    CT1 3LS. *Tel:* Canterbury (0227) 61209
Apple and pear specialists. Expert in historic varieties and will advise on
flavour. Grafts of varieties not on list may be ordered. Apples (38); Pears (13).

Pengethley Nurseries, near Harewood End, Ross-on-Wye, Hereford and
  Worcester. *Tel*: Harewood End (098 987) 284
Apples (28); Pears (4); Plums (11); Cherries (8); Peach; Quince; Mulberry;
Cob nut; Medlar; Red currant; Black currants (4); Raspberries (5); Black-
berries (2); Gooseberries (4); Blueberry; Fig.

Thomas Rivers and Son Ltd, The Nurseries, Sawbridgeworth, Hertfordshire
  CM21 0HJ. *Tel*: Bishop's Stortford (0279) 722338
The oldest nursery in Britain, with a very wide stock – many of the varieties
bred at the nursery. Apples (40); Pears (14); Plums (18); Cherries (12);
Peaches (11); Nectarines (7); Apricot; Quince (4); Medlar; Mulberry; Crab
apples (2); Walnuts (2); Cob nuts (2); Red currants (4); White currants (2);
Black currants (9); Raspberries (8); Strawberries (10); Blackberries (3);
Gooseberries (7); Loganberries (2); Figs (5); Grape vines (15); Citrus fruits (8).

R. V. Roger Ltd, The Nurseries, Pickering, North Yorkshire YO18 7HG.
  Tel: Pickering (0279) 72226
Splendid range of Lancashire gooseberries and no less than six cob nuts; good
choice in red currants too, and some alpine strawberries. Apples (38); Pears
(17); Plums (6); Cherries (9); Apricot; Crab apples (4); Red currants (7);
White currant; Quince (2); Medlar; Mulberry; Cob nuts (6); Black currants
(7); Raspberries (6); Strawberries (6); Gooseberries (50); Blackberries (3);
Loganberries (2); Fig; Grape vines (2).

Row Farm Nursery Ltd, Chapmanslade, Westbury, Wiltshire. *Tel*: Chap-
  manslade (037388) 260
Apples (21); Pears (6); Plums (9); Cherries (several); Peaches (2); Nectarine;
Apricot; Quince; Medlar; Mulberry; Cob nuts (2); Walnut; Red currant;
Black currants (3); Raspberries (4); Strawberries (5); Blackberries (2); Goose-
berries (3); Loganberry; Fig; Grape vine.

St Bridget Nurseries, Old Rydon Lane, Exeter, EX2 7JY. *Tel*: Topsham
  (039287) 3672
Apples (31); Pears (9); Plums (14); Cherries (7); Peaches (8); Nectarines (3);
Apricots (3); Quince (3); Medlar; Mulberry; Crab apples (4); Walnut; Sweet
chestnut; Red currants (2); White currant; Black currants (8); Raspberries
(5); Strawberries (3); Blackberries (3); Gooseberries (3); Loganberries (2);
Fig; Grape vines (2).

Scotts Nurseries (Merriott) Ltd, Merriott, Somerset TA16 5PL. *Tel*: Crew-
  kerne (0460) 72306
A marvellously rich list. Not included below are 17 cider apples and 13 perry
pears. Scotts can grow almost any apple in cultivation to order (using stock
from the National Fruit Trials). The catalogue notes are very informative and

useful. Apples (188); Pears (57); Plums (53); Cherries (16); Peaches (5); Nectarines (4); Apricots (3); Quince (4); Medlars (2); Mulberry; Crab apples (2); Walnut; Cob nuts (4); Chestnut; Red currants (2); White currant; Black currants (6); Raspberries (12); Strawberries (5); Blackberries (4); Gooseberries (10); Blueberries (4); Loganberries (2); Fig; Grape vines (13).

W. Seabrook and Sons Ltd, Little Leighs Hall, Little Leighs, Chelmsford CM3 1PG. *Tel:* Great Leighs (024534) 221/462
This is the Seabrook of the old blackcurrant of the same name. Advice on selection of varieties offered. Seabrook's booklet *Fruit Production in Private Gardens* (40p at time of publication) offers further help. Apples (32); Pears (14); Plums (8); Cherry; Quince; Red currants (2); White currant; Black currants (5); Loganberry.

Springhill Nurseries Ltd, Lang Stracht, Aberdeen AB2 6HY. *Tel:* Aberdeen (0224) 693788
Choice fruits for northern climates. Gooseberry varieties are notoriously difficult to identify but Springhill offers the largest selection, nearly half of the names going back a century or more. Apples (22); Pears (3); Plums (2); Cherry; Peach; Apricot; Red currant; White currant; Black currants (4); Raspberries (4); Strawberries (4); Blackberries (2); Gooseberries (52); Fig; Loganberry.

Sunningdale Nurseries, Windlesham, Surrey. *Tel:* Ascot (0990) 20496
Apples (17); Pears (5); Plums (7); Cherry; Peaches (3); Nectarines (2); Apricot; Red currants (2); White currant; Black currants (6); Gooseberries (7); Figs (2); Grape vines (2).

F. Toynbee Ltd, Croftway Nurseries, Barnham, West Sussex PO22 0BH. *Tel:* Yapton (0243) 552121
Apples (13); Pears (4); Plums (6); Cherries (4); Mulberry; Red currants (2); Black currants (3); Raspberries (6); Strawberries (7); Blackberry; Gooseberries (4); Loganberries (2); Fig; Grape vines (6).

Willik Bros Ltd, Rearsby, Liecester LE7 8YQ. *Tel:* Leicester (0533) 605515
Apples (17); Pears (4); Plums (20); Red currant; Black currant; Raspberry; Blackberry; Gooseberry; Loganberry.

Wyevale Garden Centre, King's Acre Road, Hereford. *Tel:* Hereford (0432) 65474
Apples (17); Pears (4); Plums (6); Cherries (5); Peaches (5); Nectarines (3); Apricot; Quince; Medlar; Mulberry; Walnut; Cob nuts (2); Sweet chestnut; Red currants (2); White currant; Black currants (3); Raspberries (6); Strawberries (3); Blackberries (3); Gooseberries (2); Loganberries (2); Fig; Grape vines (8).

Yeoman Gardeners Nursery and Garden Centre, 70 Newcourt Road, Topsham (039287) 3339
Apples (16); Pears (6); Plums (6); Cherries (3); Peach; Crab apples (2); Red currant; White currant; Black currants (6); Raspberries (4); Strawberries (2); Blackberries (3); Loganberry; Fig.

Other recommended nurseries:
Bees Ltd, Sealand, Chester CH1 6BA.
Blackmoor Nurseries (Cash-and-Carry), Blackmoor, Liss, Hampshire.
James Coles and Sons, Thurnby Nurseries, Leicester.
Merryweathers Garden Centre, Halam Road, Southwell, Nottinghamshire.
Notcutts Nurseries Ltd, The Nursery, Woodbridge, Suffolk.
Claude Coates Ltd, The Firs, Emneth, Wisbech, Cambridge.
G. Reuthe Ltd, Foxhill Hardy Plant Nurseries, Keston, Kent BR2 6AW.
W. C. Slocock Ltd, Goldsworth Nurseries, Alphington, Exeter, Devon.

APPENDIX II

Specialist Nurseries

Blackmoor Wholesale Fruit Nurseries, Blackmoor, Liss, Hampshire. *Tel:* Borden (04203) 3576

This interesting and highly-reputed nursery and orchard has a cash-and-carry department which is open for retail sales on Saturday mornings 9 am to 12.45 pm during the winter (November to March inclusive). The prices are very fair and there are old varieties of pears, plums, cherries, figs, cob nuts and currants, and a few apples. There is an apple shop, also run by Blackmoor Estate, from which you can buy large and small quantities of apples and other produce. This is one of the orchards which takes part in apple and pear tasting at the beginning of October; this provides a good chance to sample and compare fruits before you buy.

Family Trees, Summerlands, Curdridge, Botley, Southampton SO3 2DS. *Tel:* Botley (04892) 2026

Many nurseries stock perhaps one or two of 'family trees', with several varieties grafted on to one rootstock, but usually only with standard varieties. This nursery specialises in family trees of traditional varieties, such as Irish Peach, Orleans Reinette and Margill, or Ribston Pippin, St Edmund's Russet and Cornish Gillyflower. They also have family trees of plums, pears and cherries and a number of 'dual' fan-trained trees. This is a most exciting development for those who appreciate traditional fruits but who have only small gardens.

See also Deacons Nursery for a wide range of 'family trees'.

Frank P. Matthews Ltd, Berrington Court, Tenbury Wells, Worcestershire WR15 8TH. *Tel:* Tenbury Wells (0584) 810214

Nurserymen for the wholesale trade, this company has a superb range of varieties – but contact them only if you wish to place large orders of individual varieties. They cannot deal with small selections.

John de Putron, P.O. Box 19, St Peter Port, Guernsey, C.I. *Tel:* Guernsey (0481) 20141 and 24584

A very useful contact for many French cultivars: grafted walnuts, named almonds and peaches in particular, and two kinds of Mirabelle plum: Mirabelle de Nancy and Mirabelle de Metz. Mr de Putron is the United Kingdom representative of the great nurseries in Angers.

Read's Nursery, Loddon, Norfolk, NR14 6QW. *Tel:* Loddon (0508) 46395
An old nursery, specializing in grape vines and figs. Mulberries (2); Medlars (3); Figs (11); Grape vines (37).

James Trehane and Sons Ltd, Camellia Nursery, Stapehill Road, Hampreston,
   Wimborne, Dorset BH21 7NE
Specialists in blueberries and cranberries, with nine varieties of highbush blueberry and three of cranberry. They publish a booklet on their cultivation, available from them at a small cost.

APPENDIX III

General Information

If you have a fruit variety of uncertain identity, the best people to consult are: The Fruit Identification Department, The Royal Horticultural Society, Wisley, Ripley, Surrey. *Tel:* Ripley (048643) 3524. A small fee (50p per variety at the time of going to press) is charged.

Advice on gooseberries is available from Mr D. W. Smith, 108 Hill Cot Road, Astley Bridge, Bolton BL1 8RW. *Tel:* Bolton (0204) 54888. Mr Smith is at present working on the University of Manchester's large gooseberry collection, trying to ascertain that the varieties are correctly named. He is prepared to give advice on the identification of gooseberries and assistance with the location of older varieties and the selection of varieties for flavour.

The English Vineyards Association, The Ridge, Lamberhurst Down, Kent (*tel:* Lamberhurst (0892) 890734), hold an annual winetasting celebration in September. They also have a list of English vineyards which are open to the public and they give advice to members on the selecting and cultivation of vines for wine.

Some orchards take part in an 'apple tasting open day' which is generally held at the beginning of October. News of this is announced on local radio, and may also be obtained from the Apple and Pear Council who for a short period before the open day run a recorded telephone message with details of the orchards open to the public in various regions.

APPENDIX IV

Notes on Fruits Mentioned in this Book

The following list of fruits mentioned, grouped under their chapters, gives brief descriptions, and the nurseries from which the fruits can be obtained. For the addresses of the nurseries refer to Appendix I, where they are listed in alphabetical order.

CHAPTER TWO

Medlars

Nottingham: Fruits small but abundant. (Deacons; Highfield; Hillier; Read's; Rivers; Scotts; Wyevale)

Royal: Scarce, good flavour and cropping. (St Bridget)

Dutch: Form slightly weeping, flavour not specially good. (Jefferies; Read's; Scotts)

Quince

Portugal: Large, oblong, light orange fruits. (Allgrove; Everton; Fairfield; Goatcher; Hillier; Rivers; St Bridget; Scotts; Wyevale)

Pear-shaped: Golden-yellow fruit, good size and flavour with pruning and care. (Fairfield; Rivers; Roger)

Vranja (Bereczki): Large, pear-shaped, golden, well-flavoured fruit. (Allgrove; Aylett's; Bayley; Cheals; Harris; Highfield; Rivers; Scotts; Seabrook's)

Service (Sorbus *spp.*)

Wild Service and *Sorbus domestica:* (Hillier)

Sorbus devoniensis or *French Hales:* (Harris)

Mulberry

Morus nigra: Height when mature, 20–30 feet. For the south. (Aylett's; Cheals; Deacons; Harris; Hillier; Jackmans; Pengethley; Read's; Rivers; Roger; Row Farm; St Bridget; Scotts; Toynbee; Wyevale)

CHAPTER THREE

Apricots

Moorpark: Fruits orange with brownish-red flush, excellent flavour. (Aylett's; Boniface; Deacons; Fairfield; Goatcher; Highfield; Hillier; Jackmans; Roger; St Bridget; Scotts; Springhill; Sunningdale; Wyevale)

Hemskerk: Hardy, well-flavoured golden fruits. (Allgrove)

Shipley: Juicy well-flavoured fruits, deep yellow with a few dark red spots. (Allgrove)

Breda: Squarish fruits, deep orange with dark red flush. Slightly sharp flavour, heavy cropper. (Allgrove)

Peaches

Peregrine: Excellent flavour, good cropper; flesh juicy, greeny white. (Available from nearly every nursery on the list)

Rochester: Hardy, less well-flavoured; fruits yellow with crimson, flesh yellow. (Allgrove; Aylett's; Boniface; Bridgemere; Deacons; Goatcher; Harris; Highfield; Hillier; Rivers; Roger; St Bridget; Scotts; Sunningdale; Wyevale)

Bellegarde: Rich flavour; fruits golden and crimson; southern areas with shelter. (Allgrove)

Nectarines

Lord Napier: Rich flavour; fruits deep yellow with crimson, flesh white, juicy. (Allgrove; Aylett's; Deacons; Everton; Goatcher; Highfield; Jackmans; Rivers; St Bridget; Seabrook's; Wyevale)

Pitmaston Orange: Flavour very rich and sweet; fruit yellow with carmine; flesh golden. (Allgrove; Boniface; Goatcher; Rivers)

Elruge: Flesh white, melting, deliciously perfumed; fruit colour green/white with purplish flush. Requires wall or greenhouse. (Allgrove; Aylett's; Rivers)

Humboldt: Rich flavour; fruit golden and crimson; flesh golden; heavy cropper. (Allgrove; Rivers; St Bridget; Scotts)

Pine Apple: Yellow flesh, rich, melting flavour; colour crimson over yellow (Allgrove; Boniface; Deacons; Goatcher; Rivers; St Bridget; Scotts; Seabrook's; Wyevale)

Figs

Brown Turkey: Fruit chocolate-brown with blue tinge; flavour rich and sweet; reliable. (Listed by all *except* Bayley; Boniface; Hill; Jefferies; Keepers; New Tree; Seabrook's)

Brunswick: Large, pale green, brown-flushed fruits, flesh yellow-red, flavour excellent when well ripe. Hardy, good on walls. (Allgrove; Aylett's; Read's; Rivers; Springhill; Sunningdale)

White Marseilles: Flesh pale and transparent, very sweet and rich, fruit pale. Hardy and prolific. (Read's; Rivers)

Grapes

Black Hamburgh: Cold greenhouse grape – though it appreciates a little heat. Heavy reliable cropper. Widely stocked but flavour only fair. (Aylett's; Bridgemere; Deacons; Everton; Fairfield; Harris; Hillier; Read's; Rivers; Roger; St Bridget; Scotts; Springhill; Sunningdale; Toynbee; Wyevale)

Brant: Outdoor dessert from Canada; does well on walls. Sweet. Berries and bunches small. (Aylett's; Everton; Highfield; Jackmans; Roger; Scotts)

Chasselas d'Or (Royal Muscadine): Outdoor, on wall or under glass. Dessert or wine. Good flavour. (Jackmans; Read's; Rivers; Scotts)

Madresfield Court: Large black fruit with rich muscat flavour. Does better for heat in greenhouse. (Read's; Rivers)

Miller's Burgundy: Outdoors in a sunny sheltered place. Prolific black wine grape. (Rivers; Scotts)

Mrs Prince's Black Muscat: Black grape of excellent flavour. Greenhouse – appreciates heat at ripening time. (Highfield; Hillier; Read's; Rivers)

Muscat of Alexandria: Fine greeny-yellow greenhouse grape, ripening to amber. Needs heat to ripen to its best. (Aylett's; Bridgemere; Everton; Fairfield; Harris; Read's; Rivers; St Bridget; Sunningdale; Toynbee; Wyevale)

Muscat Hamburgh: Another grape with a fine, rich muscat flavour is also recommended. Probably a descendant of Muscat of Alexandria. Greenhouse or warm wall in the south. (Could be bought until recently and may still be available.)

Nuts

Hazelnuts (Cobnuts) and Filberts: Most nurseries list simply 'cobnuts' or Kentish Cob. Harris, Deacons, Row Farm, Scott's and Wyevale list named varieties. (Allgrove; Aylett's; Everton; Goatcher; Highfield; Hillier; Jackmans; Pengethley; Rivers; Roger)

Chestnuts: (Aylett's; Everton; Goatcher; Harris; Rogers; St Bridget; Scotts)

Walnuts: Most nurseries sell only the Common or English walnut and do not indicate a variety. Rivers stock the famous Franquette, and Hillier advertise a range of named cultivars. (Aylett's; Bridgemere; Crowder; Deacons; Fairfield; Goatcher; Highfield; Jackmans; Roger; Row Farm; St Bridget; Scotts; Wyevale)

CHAPTER FOUR

Strawberries

Royal Sovereign: Finest for flavour but susceptible to disease – make sure of certified stock. (Allgrove; Bayley; Bridgemere; Crowder; Deacons; Harris; Jackmans; Jefferies; River's; Roger; St Bridget; Scotts; Springhill; Toynbee; Wyevale; Yeoman)

Cambridge Late Pine: Good-flavoured modern strawberry which fruits into August, good disease resistance. (Harris; Hillier; Jackmans; Toynbee)

Alpine strawberries: Baron Solemacher is the one usually specified. It has excellent flavour, masses of fruit and a long season. Frais des Bois and Alexandria are sometimes available but you have to ask for them. (Hillier; Jackmans; Scotts; Toynbee). Alternatively, grow Alpine strawberries from seed. Seed merchants who are able to supply Alpine strawberries include: Suttons Seeds Ltd, Hele Road, Torquay, Devon, TQ2 7QJ. Thompson and Morgan Ltd, London Road, Ipswich, Suffolk IP2 0PA

Raspberries

Buy certified stock where possible. (Autumn fruiting and yellow varieties are not included in the scheme).

Lloyd George: Excellent flavour, heavy cropper. (Cheal; Bridgemere; Everton; Harris; Jackmans; St Bridget; Scotts; Toynbee; Wyevale; Yeoman)

Golden Everest and *Fallgold:* Two yellow raspberries – milder in taste than reds. Neither especially tasty but the only ones available. (Aylett's; Allgrove; Fairfield; Highfield; Scotts)

Malling Exploit: One of the better flavoured modern introductions. (Allgrove; Fairfield; Hill; Row Farm; Scotts)

Blackberries

Bedford Giant: Very sweet blackberry, fairly heavy cropper, very vigorous (not for the north). (Deacons; Goatcher; Highfield; Pengethley; Rivers; Roger; Seabrook's)

Himalayan Giant: Large fruit, very vigorous. Stocked by nearly every one of the nurseries listed.

John Innes: Sweet hybrid, ripens late. (Allgrove; Aylett's; Scotts)

Loganberries

Loganberry: Variety often not mentioned. Thornless (L654) and thorned (LY59) are two good clones. Stocked by nearly every nursery listed.

Red currants

Fay's Prolific: Large, sweet fruit, good for north. (Allgrove; Roger)

Raby Castle: Medium sized fruit. Prolific. (Rivers; Roger)

Wilson's Longbunch: Fruits very late. (Roger)

Red Lake: Mid season, good quality, heavy cropper. (Most nurserymen)

White currants

White Dutch: Good-flavoured fruit in long bunches, good cropper. (Allgrove; Aylett's; Rivers; St Bridget; Scotts; Sunningdale; Wyevale)

White Versailles: Large, firm, sweet fruit. Upright bush, good cropper. (Allgrove; Aylett's; Bridgemere; Cheal; Harris; Highfield; Jackmans; River's; Springhill; Yeoman)

Blackcurrants

Three good old kinds, *Seabrook's Black, Boscoop Giant* and *Baldwin* are available from almost all the listed nurseries. R. Hill in Oxfordshire has an additional *nine* varieties. (Three good modern varieties hardy and resitant to mildew are *Ben Lomond, Ben More* and *Ben Nevis.*

Gooseberries

Crown Bob: Large, culinary or dessert, claret-red fruit. Moderately good flavour. Mid-season. (Crowder)

Early Sulphur: Primrose-yellow fruit of excellent flavour. Early. (Deacons; Goatcher; Seabrook; Roger)

Golden Drop: Greeny-yellow, smallish fruit of very good flavour. Mid-season. (Harris; Rivers; Springhill)

Howard's Lancer: Pale green fruit of excellent flavour. Dessert or culinary. Mid-to late-season. (Deacons; Harris; Hill; Rivers; Roger; Scotts)

Keepsake: Large culinary or dessert fruit of very good flavour. Very pale green. (Allgrove; Deacons; Jackmans; Rivers; Roger; Scotts; Springhill; Toynbee)

Whinham's Industry: Red sweet and well-flavoured. Dessert and culinary. Does well under trees. (Allgrove; Aylett's; Bayley; Bridgemere; Cheal; Crowder; Deacons; Goatcher; Harris; Highfield; Hill; Hillier; Jackmans; Jefferies; Pengethley; Rivers; Roger; Row Farm; St Bridget; Scotts; Springhill; Toynbee; Yeoman)

Whitesmith: Excellent flavour, dessert or culinary. Pale Green, ripens to amber-white. Good all-rounder. (Allgrove; Bridgemere; Rivers; Roger; Scotts; Springhill)

Most nurseries sell the two common varieties Careless and Leveller. Aylett's have 16 varieties, Rogers 22 and Springhill 52 to choose from, including at least 20 over a century old. However, gooseberries are notoriously difficult to identify and gardeners wanting to be absolutely sure of obtaining a particular old variety may like to contact Mr D. Smith (see p. 112)

CHAPTER FIVE

Apples

NOTES Figures in brackets preceding the variety indicate the season of flowering from earliest (1) to latest (7). Ideally, pollen partners should be in the same blossom group but usually the groups before and after will overlap sufficiently to ensure pollination. The letter (t) denotes a triploid variety which requires two pollinators.

I have kept the blossom times consistent with the useful catalogue of Scotts of Merriott (other lists vary slightly) which offers the widest selection of apples. It is well worth buying; in addition to good descriptions, it gives an indication of the spread of each variety when mature.

Seasons in brackets show the period when the apple is normally ready to be eaten:

Late summer – ripening in August and early September, to be eaten at once or within ten days.

Early autumn – ripe in September, some keeping until October.

Late autumn – ripening in October, will keep until November or December in normal storage.

Midwinter – ripening in November, keeping until January or February.

New Year – ripening in December or early January, keeping until February or early March (careful storage required).

Spring – ripening in December and January, keeping until March and later (pick in late October and store carefully).

(3) *Allington Pippin:* Sharp, dessert apple which cooks well. Makes a spreading vigorous tree so not for small gardens unless grafted on to a dwarfing stock. Large lemon-yellow fruit, with red flush and faint stripes. (Late autumn)

(Allgrove; Aylett's; Bayley; Boniface; Bridgemere; Cheal; Deacon; St Bridget; Scotts; Yeoman)

(3t) *Belle de Boskoop:* Sharpish, aromatic dessert or cooking apple. Golden-yellow fruit with brick-red flush and thin russet. No good pollen. (Spring keeper.) (Allgrove)

(3t) *Blenheim Orange:* Famous dessert or cooking apple, crisp with very characteristic flavour. Fruit large, golden-yellow with faint stripe and flush of dull red, finely russetted. (Needs two other trees to pollinate it and not a good pollinator itself.) Broad spreading tree. (Midwinter) (Nearly every nursery on the list)

(3) *Calville Blanc d'Hiver (Pomme d'Api)* Fruit large, pale yellow with a pink cheek. Aromatic, tender, sweet. Not very hardy. Requires a warm summer, best on walls. (Spring) (Scotts)

(3) *Cornish Gillyflower:* Delicious, greeny-yellow apple with dull red streaks and russet, for warmer parts of the country. Slender growth and bears on branch tips. (Scotts)

(6) *Court Pendu Plat:* Smallish apple with dull red flush and slight russet. Rich flavour. Makes smallish tree, very hardy and late to blossom and fruit. (Spring) (Allgrove; Scotts)

(8) *Crawley Beauty:* Late-keeping cooking apple (introduced by Cheal); creamy yellow, striped with red. Good flavour. Flowers very late and very hardy. (Cheal; Deacons; Scotts)

(3) *D'Arcy Spice:* Greeny apple with dull red flush, covered over with russet. Rich aromatic flavour. Straggly growth. (Spring) (Rivers; Scotts; Seabrook)

(5) *French Crab:* Hard green apple with crimson flush. Excellent cooker, very long-keeping. (Scotts)

(1t) *Gravenstein:* Orange-red dessert apple with juicy, rich, aromatic flavour. Large rather sparse tree. No good as a pollinator. (Late autumn) (Allgrove; Scotts) *Gravenstein Red,* a redder bud sport.

(2) *Irish Peach:* Small, deliciously-flavoured apple, pale yellow, washed and mottled with milky-red darker stripes. Bears on tips of branches. Upright growth. (Late summer) (Scotts)

(3) *James Grieve:* Famous Scottish apple, pale creamy yellow with crimson flush and stripes, crisp and well-flavoured. Hardy. (Early autumn) (Every nursery on the list except Hill)

(5) *King of the Pippins:* Slightly bitter-sweet dessert apple, golden yellow with red-brown shading. Upright habit. Good cropper. (Allgrove; Harris; St Bridget; Scotts)

(4) *Lane's Prince Albert:* Reliable cropper, compact, spreading growth. Large, smooth, pale green fruit, striped and flushed with red. (Spring) (Nearly every nursery on the list)

(4) *Lady Sudeley:* Bright, golden-yellow fruit dashed with brilliant scarlet.

Juicy, tender and of good flavour. Compact form. (Late summer) (Allgrove; Deacons; Scotts; Springhill)

(4) *Orleans Reinette:* Golden-yellow apple with red flush and fine russet. Crisp sweet, juicy and of highest flavour. Moderate bearer; fairly large upright tree, hardy but needs protection against scab in moist climes. (New year) (Allgrove; Cheal; Deacons; Goatcher; Hillier; Keepers; Scotts)

(2t) *Ribston pippin:* One of the most richly-flavoured apples when well ripened. Crisp, yellow with brownish-red flush and some russet. Large and vigorous tree but tends to light cropping. Needs two other trees to pollinate it. (Mid-winter) (Allgrove; Cheal; Deacons; Harris; Keepers; Pengethley; Rivers; St Bridget; Scotts)

(2) *St Edmunds pippin:* Small golden russet, juicy and well-flavoured. Compact tree, good for small gardens. Crops well. Bears at tip of branches. (Early autumn) (Bridgemere; Deacons; Scotts)

(3) *Sturmer pippin:* Greeny-yellow apple, lightly russetted with excellent flavour. Fine late season dessert fruit. Hardy and crops well. Pick as late as possible. (Spring) (Allgrove; Deacons; Fairfield; Rivers; St Bridget; Scotts)

(2) *White Transparent:* Large, pale, creamy yellow dessert apple, crisp and juicy, pleasantly sharp (also cooks well). Prolific, scab resistant. Vigorous, upright tree. (Summer) (Scotts)

Crab apples

Some crab apples make good pollinators for other apples as well as being an interesting crop in their own right. Some are strictly ornamental. *John Downie, Golden Hornet* and *Dartmouth* are among the most widely-stocked which are grown for fruit as well as beauty.

(NB John Downie and several others are not subject to VAT, *ie* officially counted as fruit trees rather than ornamentals.) One or more crabs are stocked by the following nurseries:

Bayley; Bridgemere; Deacons; Fairfield; Goatcher; Hillier; Jefferies; Rivers; Roger; St Bridget; Yeoman.

CHAPTER SIX

Pears

NOTES Figures and 't' prefix – see Apple note.

The famous Williams and Comice pears are available from almost every nursery listed.

(3) *Beurre Superfin:* Yellow fruit with russet patches, one of best for flavour; moderate size for small gardens. Does not keep for long; gather in late

September and eat before it softens. Protect against scab. (October) (Scotts; Seabrook)

(4) *Doyenne du Comice:* Large golden fruit with light russet and reddish flush. Famous for flavour but unreliable in cold position or poor soil and susceptible to scab. Vigorous upright growth. (November) (Nearly every nursery listed)

(4t) *Catillac:* Very large cooking pear, remaining hard and keeping until April. Immune to scab. Vigorous growth and spreading habit. Needs two pollinators. (Allgrove; Scotts; Seabrook)

(3) *Dr Jules Guyot:* Pale gold, sometimes flushed with scarlet, flavour slightly musky. Upright growth. (Early September) (Allgrove; St Bridget; Scotts; Seabrook)

(3) *Durondeau:* Tapering, copper-red russet with red cheek. Fertile and hardy in good soils with care. (Late October–November) (Allgrove; St Bridget; Scotts; Seabrook)

(4) *Glou Morceau:* Green pear ripening slowly to pale greeny-yellow. Fertile and reliable. Sweet but needs sunny sheltered spot. (December–January) (Allgrove; Aylett's; Cheal; Roger; Rivers; Scotts; Seabrook)

(3t) *Jargonelle:* Smallish, greeny-brown tapering dessert pear, tender and juicy. Hardy, spreading growth. Needs two pollinators – Beurre Superfin good as one. (August) (Crowder; Roger; Scotts)

(3) *Josephine de Malines:* Choicest of all winter pears. Small, green fruit turning to yellow when ripe. Fertile and hardy, moderate growth for smaller gardens. Will ripen slowly over several weeks if picked when weather begins to deteriorate in October and stored carefully in cool conditions. (Allgrove; New Tree; Rivers; Scotts)

(4) *Winter Nelis:* Greeny-yellow fruit with thin dark-brown russet, juicy, sweet, delicately perfumed, with almost transparent flesh. Ripens successively and is ready for eating when still green. Moderate growth. (November –January) (Harris; Rivers; St Bridget; Scotts; Seabrook)

(3) *Black Worcester:* Large russet-brown cooking pear. (Until April) (Scotts)

CHAPTER SEVEN

Plums

NOTE For prefixed numbers see Apple note.

The Victoria plum is generally available from any nursery. The Yellow Pershore (Yellow Egg) may be had from Boniface; Crowder; Everton; Scotts and Wyevale (but this is not a plum of particularly good flavour). Other plums worth investigating are Denniston's Superb, Oullins Golden gage, and Early Transparent gage, all well-flavoured and self-fertile (Deacons; Rivers; Scotts and some others.)

Two Mirabelle plums: Mirabelle de Nancy and Mirabelle de Metz are available through John de Putron in Guernsey (see p. 110).

(3) *Bryanston gage:* Roundish gage with excellent flavour, greeny-yellow with a few red dots. Grows well as a bush or wall tree. Needs a pollinator. (September) (Everton; Scotts)

(2) *Coe's Golden Drop:* Largish, oval plum, amber-yellow with red spots. Rich, sweet flavour. Needs a sunny wall but still a shy cropper. Will not cross-pollinate with Jefferson. (Late September–October) (Allgrove; Aylett's; Bayley; Deacons; Everton; Goatacher; Rivers; Row Farm; St Bridget; Scotts; Yeoman)

(4) *Damsons – Farleigh damson:* Small, blue-black, rich flavour, heavy cropping. Needs pollinator, only partly self-fertile. Sturdy tree. (Allgrove; Harris; Scotts)

(5) *Shropshire prune: Shropshire damson:* Small, oval blue-black fruit. Exceptional flavour when cooked. Crops reliable but light. Compact upright growth. (Bayley; Crowder; Pengethley; Scotts)

(5) *Old Green gage:* Excellent flavour. Small, round, green-yellow fruit with slight red flush and russet dots. Self-infertile; not a heavy cropper, sometimes unreliable. (Late August–September) (Allgrove; Aylett's; Bayley; Boniface; Bridgemere; Deacons; Harris; Rivers; Row Farm; St Bridget; Scotts; Springhill; Sunningdale; Wyevale; Yeoman)

(1) *Jefferson:* Oval, green plum with greengage flavour. Good, hardy, needs pollinator – Denniston's Superb is good (not Coe's Golden Drop). (Mid-September) (Allgrove; Aylett's; Bayley; Everton; Goatcher; Harris; Keepers; Pengethley; Rivers; Roger; Scotts)

(3) *Golden Transparent gage (Transparent gage:)* Golden-yellow with pale violet flush and slight bloom. Flavour excellent, sweet and aromatic. Grows well on warm walls. (Needs Early Transparent gage or Denniston's Superb as pollinators: both available from Scotts.) (Early to mid-September)

(4) *Kirke's plum (Kirke's Blue:)* Large, round purple plum of good flavour. Small, spreading tree, grows well on a sunny wall, though never a heavy cropper. Best pollinated by Oullins Golden Gage. (Mid-September) (Allgrove; Everton; Highfield; Rivers; Scotts)

CHAPTER EIGHT

Cherries

Archduke: Dark red fruit, excellent flavour – refreshing for dessert, also cooks well. Partly self-fertile but better with Morello nearby. (Mid-July) (Jefferies)

Bigarreau Napoleon: Dark red fruit, good flavour. A heavy cropper but susceptible to disease. Pollinated by Frogmore Early, Waterloo, Morello, Stella (Late July) (Allgrove; Aylett's; Deacons; Everton; Goatcher; Harris; Hillier; Pengethley; Roger; Scotts)

Early Rivers: Red-black fruit, flavour delicious. A good cropper on walls. Pollinators: Merton Heart, Waterloo. (Allgrove; Aylett's; Bridgemere; Crowder; Everton; Goatcher; Hillier; Jackmans; Keepers; Rivers; St Bridget; Scotts)

Frogmore Early: Translucent yellow fruit with red flush, delicious flavour, generous crop. Pollinators: Merton Heart, Bigarreau Napoleon, Morello, Stella. (Late June) (Keepers; Rivers; St Bridget; Scotts)

Kentish Red: Shiny scarlet fruit, rather larger than Morello, juicy, slightly bitter. Pollinated by Morello. Self-fertile. (July to August) (Scotts)

May Duke: Hardy, upright tree, partly self-fertile, but better next to Morello or Archduke. Cooking or eating when fully ripe. (Scotts)

Merton Bigarreau: Fruit very dark, good flavour, heavy cropper. Large, healthy tree. Pollinated by Merton Heart, Napoleon Bigarreau, Stella, Morello. (Late June–July) (Aylett's; Boniface; Deacons; Pengethley; Rivers; Scotts)

Merton Heart: Large, fine-quality fruit, dark to black in colour. Heavy cropper. Pollinated by Early Rivers, Frogmore Early, Merton Bigarreau; Waterloo. (Late June–July) (Aylett's; Deacons; Goatcher; Scotts; Wyevale; Yeoman)

Stella: Large, dark red fruit, good flavour. Self-fertile. Good cropper. (Late July) (Aylett's; Bridgemere; Cheal; Deacons; Highfield; Pengethley; Rivers; Scotts; Wyevale)

Waterloo: Crimson fruit, sweet, rich flavour. Compact growth, good on walls. Pollinated by Merton Heart, Early Rivers, Morello. (Late June–July) (Everton; Wyevale)

Select Bibliography

The primary sources and older gardening books which I have consulted are noted in the text. This list consists of books I found particularly useful for background information. Readers wishing to go deeper into the subject, should consult the excellent bibliographies in Alicia Amherst's *A History of Gardening in England*, Eleanour Sinclair Rohde's *The Story of the Garden* (orchard and garden history) and Hyams and Jackson, *The Orchard and Garden* (fruit growing in general).

Amherst, The Lady Alicia: *A History of Gardening in England*, Quaritch, London) 1895
   (ed) *The Feate of Gardening*, Master Jon Gardener, Archaeologia LIV (pt 1) 1894
Bridge, Sir Frederick: *The Old Cryes of London*, Novello & Co., London, 1921
Bunyard, E. A.: *Handbook of Fruits*, John Murray, London, 1925
   The Anatomy of Dessert, Dulau & Co., London, 1929
Cockayne, Rev. Oswald (ed): *Leehdoms, Wortcunning and Starcraft of Early England*, H.M.S.O. 1864, reprint Kraus, 1965
Furnivall, F. J.: *Early English Meals and Manners*, Kegan, Paul, Tench, Trubner & Co., for E.E.T.S., 1868
Grubb, Norman, H.: *Cherries*, Crosby Lockwood & Co. Ltd, London, 1949
Harris, John (ed:) *The Garden*, Mitchell Beazley/New Perspectives, London, 1979
Hartley, Dorothy: *Food in England*, Macdonald & Co., London, 1954
Hyams, Edward and Jackson, A. A.: *The Orchard and Fruit Garden*, Longmans, London, 1961
Rohde, Eleanor Sinclair: *The Story of the Garden*, The Medici Society, London, 1932
   Shakespeare's Wild Flowers, The Medici Society, London, 1935
   The Old English Gardening Books, The Minerva Press, London, 1972
Taylor, H. V.: *The Plums of England*, Crosby Lockwood & Son Ltd, 1949

Recommended Gardening Books

Baker, H. A.: *Fruit*, Mitchell Beazley, London, 1980 (The Royal Horticultural Society's Encyclopaedia of Practical Gardening)
Hills, Lawrence D.: *Grow Your Own Fruit and Vegetables*, Faber, London, 1971 (paperback 1979)
Royal Horticultural Society: *The Fruit Garden Displayed*, R.H.S., 1974

INDEX